An Answer to the Question: 'What is Enlightenment?'

Immanuel Kant

1724–1804

Immanuel Kant

An Answer to the Question: 'What is Enlightenment?'

TRANSLATED BY H. B. NISBET

PENGUIN BOOKS — GREAT IDEAS

PENGUIN BOOKS

Published by the Penguin Group
Penguin Books Ltd, 80 Strand, London WC2R ORL, England
Penguin Group (USA) Inc., 375 Hudson Street, New York, New York 10014, USA
Penguin Group (Canada), 90 Eglinton Avenue East, Suite 700, Toronto, Ontario, Canada M4P 2Y3
(a division of Pearson Penguin Canada Inc.)
Penguin Ireland, 25 St Stephen's Green, Dublin 2, Ireland
(a division of Penguin Books Ltd)
Penguin Group (Australia), 250 Camberwell Road, Camberwell, Victoria 3124, Australia
(a division of Pearson Australia Group Pty Ltd)
Penguin Books India Pvt Ltd, 11 Community Centre, Panchsheel Park, New Delhi – 110 017, India
Penguin Group (NZ), 67 Apollo Drive, Rosedale, North Shore 0632, New Zealand
(a division of Pearson New Zealand Ltd)
Penguin Books (South Africa) (Pty) Ltd, 24 Sturdee Avenue,
Rosebank, Johannesburg 2196, South Africa

Penguin Books Ltd, Registered Offices: 80 Strand, London WC2R ORL, England

www.penguin.com

This selection first published in Penguin Books 2009

004

First published by Cambridge University Press 1991
Translation copyright © Cambridge University Press, 1970, 1991
All rights reserved

All pieces in this collection taken from Kant's *Political Writings*, edited by H. S. Reiss and
translated by H. B. Nisbet. This reprint edition is published with the permission of the Syndicate of
the Press of the University of Cambridge, Cambridge, England

Set by Rowland Phototypesetting Ltd, Bury St Edmunds, Suffolk
Printed in England by Clays Ltd, St Ives plc

978–0–141–04388–3

www.greenpenguin.co.uk

FSC
www.fsc.org

MIX
Paper from
responsible sources
FSC™ C018179

Penguin Books is committed to a sustainable
future for our business, our readers and our planet.
This book is made from Forest Stewardship
Council™ certified paper.

Contents

An Answer to the Question: 'What is Enlightenment?'

Enlightenment is man's emergence from his self-incurred immaturity. Immaturity is the inability to use one's own understanding without the guidance of another. This immaturity is *self-incurred* if its cause is not lack of understanding, but lack of resolution and courage to use it without the guidance of another. The motto of enlightenment is therefore: *Sapere aude!* [Dare to be wise!] Have courage to use your *own* understanding!

Laziness and cowardice are the reasons why such a large proportion of men, even when nature has long emancipated them from alien guidance (*naturaliter maiorennes* [Those who have come of age by virtue of nature]), nevertheless gladly remain immature for life. For the same reasons, it is all too easy for others to set themselves up as their guardians. It is so convenient to be immature! If I have a book to have understanding in place of me, a spiritual adviser to have a conscience for me, a doctor to judge my diet for me, and so on, I need not make any efforts at all. I need not think, so long as I can pay; others will soon enough take the tiresome job over for me. The guardians who have kindly taken upon themselves the work of supervision will soon see to it that by far the largest part of mankind (including the entire fair sex) should consider the step forward to maturity not only as difficult but also as highly dangerous. Having first infatuated their domesticated animals, and carefully prevented the docile creatures from daring to take a single step without the leading-strings to which they are tied, they next show them the danger which threatens them if they try to walk unaided. Now this danger is not in fact so very great, for they would certainly learn to walk eventually after a few falls. But an example of this kind is intimidating, and usually frightens them off from further attempts.

Thus it is difficult for each separate individual to work his way out of the immaturity which has become almost second nature to him. He has even grown fond of it and is really incapable for the time being of using his own understanding, because he was never allowed to make the attempt. Dogmas and formulas, those mechanical instruments for rational use (or rather misuse) of his natural endowments, are the ball and chain of his permanent immaturity. And if anyone did throw them off, he would still be uncertain about jumping over even the narrowest of trenches, for he would be unaccustomed to free movement of this kind. Thus only a few, by cultivating their own minds, have succeeded in freeing themselves from immaturity and in continuing boldly on their way.

There is more chance of an entire public enlightening itself. This is indeed almost inevitable, if only the public concerned is left in freedom. For there will always be a few who think for themselves, even among those appointed as guardians of the common mass. Such guardians, once they have themselves thrown off the yoke of immaturity, will disseminate the spirit of rational respect for personal value and for the duty of all men to think for themselves. The remarkable thing about this is that if the public, which was previously put under this yoke by the guardians, is suitably stirred up by some of the latter who are incapable of enlightenment, it may subsequently compel the guardians themselves to remain under the yoke. For it is very harmful to propagate prejudices, because they finally avenge themselves on the very people who first encouraged them (or whose predecessors did so). Thus a public can only achieve enlightenment slowly. A revolution may well put an end to autocratic despotism and to rapacious or power-seeking oppression, but it will never produce a true reform in ways of thinking. Instead, new prejudices, like the ones they replaced, will serve as a leash to control the great unthinking mass.

For enlightenment of this kind, all that is needed is *freedom*. And the freedom in question is the most innocuous form of all – freedom to make *public use* of one's reason in all matters. But I hear on all sides the cry: *Don't argue!* The officer says: Don't argue, get on parade! The tax-official: Don't argue, pay! The clergyman: Don't argue, believe! (Only one ruler in the world says: *Argue* as much as you like and about whatever you like, *but obey*!) All this means restrictions on freedom everywhere. But which sort of restriction prevents enlightenment, and which, instead of hindering it, can actually promote it? I reply: The *public use* of man's reason must always be free, and it alone can bring about enlightenment among men; the *private use* of reason may quite often be very narrowly restricted, however, without undue hindrance to the progress of enlightenment. But by the public use of one's own reason I mean that use which anyone may make of it *as a man of learning* addressing the entire *reading public*. What I term the private use of reason is that which a person may make of it in a particular *civil* post or office with which he is entrusted.

Now in some affairs which affect the interests of the commonwealth, we require a certain mechanism whereby some members of the commonwealth must behave purely passively, so that they may, by an artificial common agreement, be employed by the government for public ends (or at least deterred from vitiating them). It is, of course, impermissible to argue in such cases; obedience is imperative. But in so far as this or that individual who acts as part of the machine also considers himself as a member of a complete commonwealth or even of cosmopolitan society, and thence as a man of learning who may through his writings address a public in the truest sense of the word, he may indeed argue without harming the affairs in which he is employed for some of the time in a passive capacity. Thus it would be very harmful if an officer receiving an order from his superiors were to quibble openly, while on duty, about the appropriateness or usefulness of the order in question. He must simply obey. But he cannot reasonably be banned from making observations as a man of learning on the errors in the military service, and from submitting these to his public for judgement. The citizen cannot refuse to pay the taxes imposed upon him; presumptuous criticisms of such taxes, where someone is called upon to pay them, may be punished as an outrage which could lead to general insubordination. Nonetheless, the same citizen does not contravene his civil obligations if, as a learned individual, he publicly voices his thoughts on the impropriety or even injustice of such fiscal measures. In the same way, a clergyman is bound to instruct his pupils and his congregation in accordance with the doctrines of the church he serves, for he was employed by it on that condition. But as a scholar, he is completely free as well as obliged to impart to the public all his carefully considered, well-intentioned thoughts on the mistaken aspects of those doctrines, and to offer suggestions for a better arrangement of religious and ecclesiastical affairs. And there is nothing in this which need trouble the conscience. For what he teaches in pursuit of his duties as an active servant of the church is presented by him as something which he is not empowered to teach at his own discretion, but which he is employed to expound in a prescribed manner and in someone else's name. He will say: Our church teaches this or that, and these are the arguments it uses. He then extracts as much practical value as possible for his congregation from precepts to which he would not himself subscribe with full conviction, but which he can nevertheless undertake to expound, since it is not in fact wholly impossible that they may contain truth. At all events, nothing opposed to the essence of religion is present in such doctrines. For if the clergyman thought he could find anything of this sort in them, he would not be able to carry out his official duties in good conscience, and would have to resign. Thus the use which someone employed as a teacher makes of his reason in the presence of his congregation is purely *private*, since a congregation, however large it is, is never any more than a domestic gathering. In view of this, he is not and cannot be free as a priest, since he is acting on a commission imposed from outside. Conversely, as a scholar addressing the real public (i.e. the world at large) through his writings, the clergyman making *public use* of his reason enjoys unlimited freedom to use his own reason and to speak in his own person. For to maintain that the guardians of the people in spiritual matters should themselves be immature, is an absurdity which amounts to making absurdities permanent.

But should not a society of clergymen, for example an ecclesiastical synod or a venerable presbytery (as the Dutch call it), be entitled to commit itself by oath to a certain unalterable set of doctrines, in order to secure for all time a constant guardianship over each of its members, and through them over the people? I reply that this is quite impossible. A contract of this kind, concluded with a view to preventing all further enlightenment of mankind for ever, is absolutely null and void, even if it is ratified by the supreme power, by Imperial Diets and the most solemn peace treaties. One age cannot enter into an alliance on oath to put the next age in a position where it would be impossible for it to extend and correct its knowledge, particularly on such important matters, or to make any progress whatsoever in enlightenment. This would be a crime against human nature, whose original destiny lies precisely in such progress.

Later generations are thus perfectly entitled to dismiss these agreements as unauthorized and criminal. To test whether any particular measure can be agreed upon as a law for a people, we need only ask whether a people could well impose such a law upon itself. This might well be possible for a specified short period as a means of introducing a certain order, pending, as it were, a better solution. This would also mean that each citizen, particularly the clergyman, would be given a free hand as a scholar to comment publicly, i.e. in his writings, on the inadequacies of current institutions. Meanwhile, the newly established order would continue to exist, until public insight into the nature of such matters had progressed and proved itself to the point where, by general consent (if not unanimously), a proposal could be submitted to the crown. This would seek to protect the congregations who had, for instance, agreed to alter their religious establishment in accordance with their own notions of what higher insight is, but it would not try to obstruct those who wanted to let things remain as before. But it is absolutely impermissible to agree, even for a single lifetime, to a permanent religious constitution which no one might publicly question. For this would virtually nullify a phase in man's upward progress, thus making it fruitless and even detrimental to subsequent generations. A man may for his own person, and even then only for a limited period, postpone enlightening himself in matters he ought to know about. But to renounce such enlightenment completely, whether for his own person or even more so for later generations, means violating and trampling underfoot the sacred rights of mankind. But something which a people may not even impose upon itself can still less be imposed on it by a monarch; for his legislative authority depends precisely upon his uniting the collective will of the people in his own. So long as he sees to it that all true or imagined improvements are compatible with the civil order, he can otherwise leave his subjects to do whatever they find necessary for their salvation, which is none of his business. But it is his business to stop anyone forcibly hindering others from working as best they can to define and promote their salvation. It indeed detracts from his majesty if he interferes in these affairs by subjecting the writings in which his subjects attempt to clarify their religious ideas to governmental supervision. This applies if he does so acting upon his own exalted opinions – in which case he exposes himself to the reproach: *Caesar non est supra Grammaticos* [Caesar is not above the Grammarians] – but much more so if he demeans his high authority so far as to support the spiritual despotism of a few tyrants within his state against the rest of his subjects.

If it is now asked whether we at present live in an *enlightened* age, the answer is: No, but we do live in an age of *enlightenment*. As things are at present, we still have a long way to go before men as a whole can be in a position (or can even be put into a position) of using their own understanding confidently and well in religious matters, without outside guidance. But we do have distinct indications that the way is now being cleared for them to work freely in this direction, and that the obstacles to universal enlightenment, to man's emergence from his self-incurred immaturity, are gradually becoming fewer. In this respect our age is the age of enlightenment, the century of *Frederick*.

A prince who does not regard it as beneath him to say that he considers it his duty, in religious matters, not to prescribe anything to his people, but to allow them complete freedom, a prince who thus even declines to accept the presumptuous title of *tolerant*, is himself enlightened. He deserves to be praised by a grateful present and posterity as the man who first liberated mankind from immaturity (as far as government is concerned), and who left all men free to use their own reason in all matters of conscience. Under his rule, ecclesiastical dignitaries, notwithstanding their official duties, may in their capacity as scholars freely and publicly submit to the judgement of the world their verdicts and opinions, even if these deviate here and there from orthodox doctrine. This applies even more to all others who are not restricted by any official duties. This spirit of freedom is also spreading abroad, even where it has to struggle with outward obstacles imposed by governments which misunderstand their own function. For such governments can now witness a shining example of how freedom may exist without in the least jeopardizing public concord and the unity of the commonwealth. Men will of their own accord gradually work their way out of barbarism so long as artificial measures are not deliberately adopted to keep them in it.

I have portrayed *matters of religion* as the focal point of enlightenment, i.e. of man's emergence from his self-incurred immaturity. This is firstly because our rulers have no interest in assuming the role of guardians over their subjects so far as the arts and sciences are concerned, and secondly, because religious immaturity is the most pernicious and dishonourable variety of all. But the attitude of mind of a head of state who favours freedom in the arts and sciences extends even further, for he realizes that there is no danger even to his *legislation* if he allows his subjects to make *public use* of their own reason and to put before the public their thoughts on better ways of drawing up laws, even if this entails forthright criticism of the current legislation. We have before us a brilliant example of this kind, in which no monarch has yet surpassed the one to whom we now pay tribute.

But only a ruler who is himself enlightened and has no fear of phantoms, yet who likewise has at hand a well-disciplined and numerous army to guarantee public security, may say what no republic would dare to say: *Argue as much as you like and about whatever you like, but obey!* This reveals to us a strange and unexpected pattern in human affairs (such as we shall always find if we consider them in the widest sense, in which nearly everything is paradoxical). A high degree of civil freedom seems advantageous to a people's *intellectual* freedom, yet it also sets up insuperable barriers to it. Conversely, a lesser degree of civil freedom gives intellectual freedom enough room to expand to its fullest extent. Thus once the germ on which nature has lavished most care – man's inclination and vocation to *think freely* – has developed within this hard shell, it gradually reacts upon the mentality of the people, who thus gradually become increasingly able to *act freely*. Eventually, it even influences the principles of governments, which find that they can themselves profit by treating man, who is *more than a machine*, in a manner appropriate to his dignity.[1]

Königsberg in Prussia, 30th September, 1784.

Perpetual Peace:
A Philosophical Sketch

'The Perpetual Peace'

A Dutch innkeeper once put this satirical inscription on his signboard, along with the picture of a graveyard. We shall not trouble to ask whether it applies to men in general, or particularly to heads of state (who can never have enough of war), or only to the philosophers who blissfully dream of perpetual peace. The author of the present essay does, however, make one reservation in advance. The practical politician tends to look down with great complacency upon the political theorist as a mere academic. The theorist's abstract ideas, the practitioner believes, cannot endanger the state, since the state must be founded upon principles of experience; it thus seems safe to let him fire off his whole broadside, and the *worldly-wise* statesman need not turn a hair. It thus follows that if the practical politician is to be consistent, he must not claim, in the event of a dispute with the theorist, to scent any danger to the state in the opinions which the theorist has randomly uttered in public. By this saving clause, the author of this essay will consider himself expressly safeguarded, in correct and proper style, against all malicious interpretation.

*Which Contains the Preliminary Articles of a Perpetual
Peace Between States*

1. 'No conclusion of peace shall be considered valid as
such if it was made with a secret reservation of the
material for a future war.'

For if this were the case, it would be a mere truce, a suspension of hostilities, not a *peace*. Peace means an end to
all hostilities, and to attach the adjective 'perpetual' to it
is already suspiciously close to pleonasm. A conclusion of
peace nullifies all existing reasons for a future war, even if
these are not yet known to the contracting parties, and no
matter how acutely and carefully they may later be pieced
together out of old documents. It is possible that either
party may make a mental reservation with a view to re-
viving its old pretensions in the future. Such reservations
will not be mentioned explicitly, since both parties may
simply be too exhausted to continue the war, although
they may nonetheless possess sufficient ill will to seize
the first favourable opportunity of attaining their end.
But if we consider such reservations in themselves, they
soon appear as Jesuitical casuistry; they are beneath the
dignity of a ruler, just as it is beneath the dignity of a minister of state to comply with any reasoning of this kind.

But if, in accordance with 'enlightened' notions of
political expediency, we believe that the true glory of a
state consists in the constant increase of its power by any
means whatsoever, the above judgement will certainly
appear academic and pedantic.

2. 'No independently existing state, whether it be large or small, may be acquired by another state by inheritance, exchange, purchase or gift.'

For a state, unlike the ground on which it is based, is not a possession (*patrimonium*). It is a society of men, which no one other than itself can command or dispose of. Like a tree, it has its own roots, and to graft it on to another state as if it were a shoot is to terminate its existence as a moral personality and make it into a commodity. This contradicts the idea of the original contract, without which the rights of a people are unthinkable.[2] Everyone knows what danger the supposed right of acquiring states in this way, even in our own times, has brought upon Europe (for this practice is unknown in other continents). It has been thought that states can marry one another, and this has provided a new kind of industry by which power can be increased through family alliances, without expenditure of energy, while landed property can be extended at the same time. It is the same thing when the troops of one state are hired to another to fight an enemy who is not common to both; for the subjects are thereby used and misused as objects to be manipulated at will.

3. 'Standing armies (*miles perpetuus*) will gradually be abolished altogether.'

For they constantly threaten other states with war by the very fact that they are always prepared for it. They spur on the states to outdo one another in arming unlimited numbers of soldiers, and since the resultant costs eventually make peace more oppressive than a short war, the armies are themselves the cause of wars of aggression which set out to end burdensome military expenditure. Furthermore, the hiring of men to kill or to be killed seems to mean using them as mere machines and instruments in the hands of someone else (the state), which cannot easily be reconciled with the rights of man in one's own person. It is quite a different matter if the citizens undertake voluntary military training from time to time in order to secure themselves and their fatherland against attacks from outside. But it would be just the same if wealth rather than soldiers were accumulated, for it would be seen by other states as a military threat; it might compel them to mount preventive attacks, for of the three powers within a state – the *power of the army*, the *power of alliance* and the *power of money* – the third is probably the most reliable instrument of war. It would lead more often to wars if it were not so difficult to discover the amount of wealth which another state possesses.

4. 'No national debt shall be contracted in connection with the external affairs of the state.'

There is no cause for suspicion if help for the national economy is sought inside or outside the state (e.g. for improvements to roads, new settlements, storage of food-stuffs for years of famine, etc.). But a credit system, if used by the powers as an instrument of aggression against one another, shows the power of money in its most dangerous form. For while the debts thereby incurred are always secure against present demands (because not all the creditors will demand payment at the same time), these debts go on growing indefinitely. This ingenious system, invented by a commercial people in the present century, provides a military fund which may exceed the resources of all the other states put together. It can only be exhausted by an eventual tax-deficit, which may be postponed for a considerable time by the commercial stimulus which industry and trade receive through the credit system. This ease in making war, coupled with the warlike inclination of those in power (which seems to be an integral feature of human nature), is thus a great obstacle in the way of perpetual peace. Foreign debts must therefore be prohibited by a preliminary article of such a peace, otherwise national bankruptcy, inevitable in the long run, would necessarily involve various other states in the resultant loss without their having deserved it, thus inflicting upon them a public injury. Other states are therefore justified in allying themselves against such a state and its pretensions.

5. 'No state shall forcibly interfere in the constitution and government of another state.'

For what could justify such interference? Surely not any sense of scandal or offence which a state arouses in the subjects of another state. It should rather serve as a warning to others, as an example of the great evils which a people has incurred by its lawlessness. And a bad example which one free person gives to another (as a *scandalum acceptum*) is not the same as an injury to the latter. But it would be a different matter if a state, through internal discord, were to split into two parts, each of which set itself up as a separate state and claimed authority over the whole. For it could not be reckoned as interference in another state's constitution if an external state were to lend support to one of them, because their condition is one of anarchy. But as long as this internal conflict is not yet decided, the interference of external powers would be a violation of the rights of an independent people which is merely struggling with its internal ills. Such interference would be an active offence and would make the autonomy of all other states insecure.

6. 'No state at war with another shall permit such acts of hostility as would make mutual confidence impossible during a future time of peace. Such acts would include the employment of *assassins* (*percussores*) or poisoners (*venefici*), *breach of agreements, the instigation of treason* (*perduellio*) within the enemy state, etc.'

These are dishonourable stratagems. For it must still remain possible, even in wartime, to have some sort of trust in the attitude of the enemy, otherwise peace could not be concluded and the hostilities would turn into a war of extermination (*bellum internecinum*). After all, war is only a regrettable expedient for asserting one's rights by force within a state of nature, where no court of justice is available to judge with legal authority. In such cases, neither party can be declared an unjust enemy, for this would already presuppose a judge's decision; only the *outcome* of the conflict, as in the case of a so-called 'judgement of God', can decide who is in the right. A war of punishment (*bellum punitivum*) between states is inconceivable, since there can be no relationship of superior to inferior among them. It thus follows that a war of extermination, in which both parties and right itself might all be simultaneously annihilated, would allow perpetual peace only on the vast graveyard of the human race. A war of this kind and the employment of all means which might bring it about must thus be absolutely prohibited. But the means listed above would inevitably lead to such a war, because these diabolical arts, besides being intrinsically despicable, would not long be confined to war alone if they were brought into use. This applies, for example, to the employment of spies (*uti exploratoribus*), for it exploits only the dishonesty of others (which can never be completely eliminated). Such practices will be carried over into peacetime and will thus completely vitiate its purpose.

All of the articles listed above, when regarded objectively or in relation to the intentions of those in power, are *prohibitive laws* (*leges prohibitivae*). Yet some of them are of the *strictest* sort (*leges strictae*), being valid irrespective of differing circumstances, and they require that the abuses they prohibit should be abolished *immediately* (Nos. 1, 5 and 6). Others (Nos. 2, 3 and 4), although they are not exceptions to the rule of justice, allow some *subjective* latitude according to the circumstances in which they are applied (*leges latae*). The latter need not necessarily be executed at once, so long as their ultimate purpose (e.g. the *restoration* of freedom to certain states in accordance with the second article) is not lost sight of. But their execution may not be *put off* to a non-existent date (*ad calendas graecas*, as Augustus used to promise), for any delay is permitted only as a means of avoiding a premature implementation which might frustrate the whole purpose of the article. For in the case of the second article, the prohibition relates only to the *mode of acquisition*, which is to be forbidden hereforth, but not to the present *state of political possessions*. For although this present state is not backed up by the requisite legal authority, it was considered lawful in the public opinion of every state at the time of the putative acquisition.[3]

SECOND SECTION

Which Contains the Definitive Articles of a Perpetual Peace Between States

A state of peace among men living together is not the same as the state of nature, which is rather a state of war. For even if it does not involve active hostilities, it involves a constant threat of their breaking out. Thus the state of peace must be *formally instituted*, for a suspension of hostilities is not in itself a guarantee of peace. And unless one neighbour gives a guarantee to the other at his request (which can happen only in a *lawful* state), the latter may treat him as an enemy.[4]

First Definitive Article of a Perpetual Peace: The Civil Constitution of Every State shall be Republican

A *republican constitution* is founded upon three principles: firstly, the principle of *freedom* for all members of a society (as men); secondly, the principle of the *dependence* of everyone upon a single common legislation (as subjects); and thirdly, the principle of legal *equality* for everyone (as citizens).[5] It is the only constitution which can be derived from the idea of an original contract, upon which all rightful legislation of a people must be founded. Thus as far as right is concerned, republicanism is in itself the original basis of every kind of civil constitution, and it only remains to ask whether it is the only constitution which can lead to a perpetual peace.

The republican constitution is not only pure in its origin (since it springs from the pure concept of right); it also offers a prospect of attaining the desired result, i.e. a perpetual peace, and the reason for this is as follows. – If, as is inevitably the case under this constitution, the consent of the citizens is required to decide whether or not war is to be declared, it is very natural that they will have great hesitation in embarking on so dangerous an enterprise. For this would mean calling down on themselves all the miseries of war, such as doing the fighting themselves, supplying the costs of the war from their own resources, painfully making good the ensuing devastation, and, as the crowning evil, having to take upon themselves a burden of debt which will embitter peace itself and which can never be paid off on account of the constant threat of new wars. But under a constitution where the subject is not a citizen, and which is therefore not republican, it is the simplest thing in the world to go to war. For the head of state is not a fellow citizen, but the owner of the state, and a war will not force him to make the slightest sacrifice so far as his banquets, hunts, pleasure palaces and court festivals are concerned. He can thus decide on war, without any significant reason, as a kind of amusement, and unconcernedly leave it to the diplomatic corps (who are always ready for such purposes) to justify the war for the sake of propriety.

The following remarks are necessary to prevent the republican constitution from being confused with the democratic one, as commonly happens. The various forms of state (*civitas*) may be classified either according to the different persons who exercise supreme authority, or according to the way in which the nation is governed by its ruler, whoever he may be. The first classification goes by the form of sovereignty (*forma imperii*), and only three such forms are possible, depending on whether the ruling power is in the hands of an *individual*, of *several persons* in association, or of *all* those who together constitute civil society (i.e. *autocracy, aristocracy* and *democracy* – the power of a prince, the power of a nobility, and the power of the people). The second classification depends on the form of government (*forma regiminis*), and relates to the way in which the state, setting out from its constitution (i.e. an act of the general will whereby the mass becomes a people), makes use of its plenary power. The form of government, in this case, will be either *republican* or *despotic*. *Republicanism* is that political principle whereby the executive power (the government) is separated from the legislative power. Despotism prevails in a state if the laws are made and arbitrarily executed by one and the same power, and it reflects the will of the people only in so far as the ruler treats the will of the people as his own private will. Of the three forms of sovereignty, *democracy*, in the truest sense of the word, is necessarily a *despotism*, because it establishes an executive power through which all the citizens may make decisions about (and indeed against) the single individual without his consent, so that decisions are made by all the people and yet not by all the people; and this means that the general will is in contradiction with itself, and thus also with freedom.

For any form of government which is not *representative* is essentially an *anomaly*, because one and the same person cannot at the same time be both the legislator and the executor of his own will, just as the general proposition in logical reasoning cannot at the same time be a secondary proposition subsuming the particular within the general. And even if the other two political constitutions (i.e. autocracy and aristocracy) are always defective in as much as they leave room for a despotic form of government, it is at least possible that they will be associated with a form of government which accords with the *spirit* of a representative system. Thus Frederick II at least *said* that he was merely the highest servant of the state,[6] while a democratic constitution makes this attitude impossible, because everyone under it wants to be a ruler. We can therefore say that the smaller the number of ruling persons in a state and the greater their powers of representation, the more the constitution will approximate to its republican potentiality, which it may hope to realize eventually by gradual reforms. For this reason, it is more difficult in an aristocracy than in a monarchy to reach this one and only perfectly lawful kind of constitution, while it is possible in a democracy only by means of violent revolution. But the people are immensely more concerned with the mode of government[7] than with the form of the constitution, although a great deal also depends on the degree to which the constitution fits the purpose of the government. But if the mode of government is to accord with the concept of right, it must be based on the representative system. This system alone makes possible a republican state, and without it, despotism and violence will result, no matter what kind of constitution is in force. None of the so-called 'republics' of antiquity employed such a system, and they thus inevitably ended in despotism, although this is still relatively bearable under the rule of a single individual.

Second Definitive Article of a Perpetual Peace: The Right of Nations shall be based on a Federation of Free States

Peoples who have grouped themselves into nation states may be judged in the same way as individual men living in a state of nature, independent of external laws; for they are a standing offence to one another by the very fact that they are neighbours. Each nation, for the sake of its own security, can and ought to demand of the others that they should enter along with it into a constitution, similar to the civil one, within which the rights of each could be secured. This would mean establishing a *federation of peoples*. But a federation of this sort would not be the same thing as an international state. For the idea of an international state is contradictory, since every state involves a relationship between a superior (the legislator) and an inferior (the people obeying the laws), whereas a number of nations forming one state would constitute a single nation. And this contradicts our initial assumption, as we are here considering the right of nations in relation to one another in so far as they are a group of separate states which are not to be welded together as a unit.

We look with profound contempt upon the way in which savages cling to their lawless freedom. They would rather engage in incessant strife than submit to a legal constraint which they might impose upon themselves, for they prefer the freedom of folly to the freedom of reason. We regard this as barbarism, coarseness, and brutish debasement of humanity. We might thus expect that civilized peoples, each united within itself as a state, would hasten to abandon so degrading a condition as soon as possible. But instead of doing so, each *state* sees its own majesty (for it would be absurd to speak of the majesty of a *people*) precisely in not having to submit to any external legal constraint, and the glory of its ruler consists in his power to order thousands of people to immolate themselves for a cause which does not truly concern them, while he need not himself incur any danger whatsoever.[8] And the main difference between the savage nations of Europe and those of America is that while some American tribes have been entirely eaten up by their enemies, the Europeans know how to make better use of those they have defeated than merely by making a meal of them. They would rather use them to increase the number of their own subjects, thereby augmenting their stock of instruments for conducting even more extensive wars.

Although it is largely concealed by governmental constraints in law-governed civil society, the depravity of human nature is displayed without disguise in the unrestricted relations which obtain between the various nations. It is therefore to be wondered at that the word *right* has not been completely banished from military politics as superfluous pedantry, and that no state has been bold enough to declare itself publicly in favour of doing so. For Hugo Grotius, Pufendorf, Vattel and the rest (sorry comforters as they are) are still dutifully quoted in *justification* of military aggression, although their philosophically or diplomatically formulated codes do not and cannot have the slightest *legal* force, since states as such are not subject to a common external constraint. Yet there is no instance of a state ever having been moved to desist from its purpose by arguments supported by the testimonies of such notable men. This homage which every state pays (in words at least) to the concept of right proves that man possesses a greater moral capacity, still dormant at present, to overcome eventually the evil principle within him (for he cannot deny that it exists), and to hope that others will do likewise. Otherwise the word *right* would never be used by states which intend to make war on one another, unless in a derisory sense, as when a certain Gallic prince declared: 'Nature has given to the strong the prerogative of making the weak obey them.' The way in which states seek their rights can only be by war, since there is no external tribunal to put their claims to trial. But rights cannot be decided by military victory, and a *peace treaty* may put an end to the current war, but not to that general warlike condition within which pretexts can always be found for a new war. And indeed, such a state of affairs cannot be pronounced completely unjust, since it allows each party to act as judge in its own cause. Yet while natural right allows us to say of men living in a lawless condition that they ought to abandon it, the right of nations does not allow us to say the same of states. For as states, they already have a lawful internal constitution, and have thus outgrown the coercive right of others to subject them to a wider legal constitution in accordance with their conception of right. On the other hand, reason, as the highest legislative moral power, absolutely condemns war as a test of rights and sets up peace as an immediate duty. But peace can neither be inaugurated nor secured without a general agreement between the nations; thus a particular kind of league, which we might call a *pacific federation* (*foedus pacificum*), is required. It would differ from a *peace treaty* (*pactum pacis*) in that the latter terminates *one* war, whereas the former would seek to end *all* wars for good. This federation does not aim to acquire any power like that of a state, but merely to preserve and secure the *freedom* of each state in itself, along with that of the other confederated states, although this does not mean that they need to submit to public laws and to a coercive power which enforces them, as do men in a state of nature. It can be shown that this idea of *federalism*, extending gradually to encompass all states and thus leading to perpetual peace, is practicable and has objective reality. For if by good fortune one powerful and enlightened nation can form a republic (which is by its nature inclined to seek perpetual peace), this will provide a focal point for federal association among other states. These will join up with the first one, thus securing the freedom of each state in accordance with the idea of international right, and the whole will gradually spread further and further by a series of alliances of this kind.

It would be understandable for a people to say: 'There shall be no war among us; for we will form ourselves into a state, appointing for ourselves a supreme legislative, executive and juridical power to resolve our conflicts by peaceful means.' But if this state says: 'There shall be no war between myself and other states, although I do not recognize any supreme legislative power which could secure my rights and whose rights I should in turn secure', it is impossible to understand what justification I can have for placing any confidence in my rights, unless I can rely on some substitute for the union of civil society, i.e. on a free federation. If the concept of international right is to retain any meaning at all, reason must necessarily couple it with a federation of this kind.

The concept of international right becomes meaningless if interpreted as a right to go to war. For this would make it a right to determine what is lawful not by means of universally valid external laws, but by means of one-sided maxims backed up by physical force. It could be taken to mean that it is perfectly just for men who adopt this attitude to destroy one another, and thus to find perpetual peace in the vast grave where all the horrors of violence and those responsible for them would be buried. There is only one rational way in which states coexisting with other states can emerge from the lawless condition of pure warfare. Just like individual men, they must renounce their savage and lawless freedom, adapt themselves to public coercive laws, and thus form an *international state* (*civitas gentium*), which would necessarily continue to grow until it embraced all the peoples of the earth. But since this is not the will of the nations, according to their present conception of international right (so that they reject *in hypothesi* what is true *in thesi*), the positive idea of a *world republic* cannot be realized. If all is not to be lost, this can at best find a negative substitute in the shape of an enduring and gradually expanding *federation* likely to prevent war. The latter may check the current of man's inclination to defy the law and antagonize his fellows, although there will always be a risk of it bursting forth anew. *Furor impius intus – fremit horridus ore cruento* (Virgil) ['Wicked Frenzy rages savagely with blood-stained mouth'].[9]

Third Definitive Article of a Perpetual Peace: Cosmopolitan Right shall be limited to Conditions of Universal Hospitality

As in the foregoing articles, we are here concerned not with philanthropy, but with *right*. In this context, *hospitality* means the right of a stranger not to be treated with hostility when he arrives on someone else's territory. He can indeed be turned away, if this can be done without causing his death, but he must not be treated with hostility, so long as he behaves in a peaceable manner in the place he happens to be in. The stranger cannot claim the *right of a guest* to be entertained, for this would require a special friendly agreement whereby he might become a member of the native household for a certain time. He may only claim a *right of resort*, for all men are entitled to present themselves in the society of others by virtue of their right to communal possession of the earth's surface. Since the earth is a globe, they cannot disperse over an infinite area, but must necessarily tolerate one another's company. And no one originally has any greater right than anyone else to occupy any particular portion of the earth. The community of man is divided by uninhabitable parts of the earth's surface such as oceans and deserts, but even then, the *ship* or the *camel* (the ship of the desert) make it possible for them to approach their fellows over these ownerless tracts, and to utilize as a means of social intercourse that *right to the earth's surface* which the human race shares in common. The inhospitable behaviour of coastal dwellers (as on the Barbary coast) in plundering ships on the adjoining seas or enslaving stranded seafarers, or that of inhabitants of the desert (as with the Arab Bedouins), who regard their proximity to nomadic tribes as a justification for plundering them, is contrary to natural right. But this natural right of hospitality, i.e. the right of strangers, does not extend beyond those conditions which make it possible for them to *attempt* to enter into relations with the native inhabitants. In this way, continents distant from each other can enter into peaceful mutual relations which may eventually be regulated by public laws, thus bringing the human race nearer and nearer to a cosmopolitan constitution.

If we compare with this ultimate end the *inhospitable* conduct of the civilized states of our continent, especially the commercial states, the injustice which they display in *visiting* foreign countries and peoples (which in their case is the same as *conquering* them) seems appallingly great. America, the negro countries, the Spice Islands, the Cape, etc. were looked upon at the time of their discovery as ownerless territories; for the native inhabitants were counted as nothing. In East India (Hindustan), foreign troops were brought in under the pretext of merely setting up trading posts. This led to oppression of the natives, incitement of the various Indian states to widespread wars, famine, insurrection, treachery and the whole litany of evils which can afflict the human race.

China[10] and Japan (Nippon), having had experience of such guests, have wisely placed restrictions on them. China permits contact with her territories, but not entrance into them, while Japan only allows contact with a single European people, the Dutch, although they are still segregated from the native community like prisoners. The worst (or, from the point of view of moral judgements, the best) thing about all this is that the commercial states do not even benefit by their violence, for all their trading companies are on the point of collapse. The Sugar Islands, that stronghold of the cruellest and most calculated slavery, do not yield any real profit;

they serve only the indirect (and not entirely laudable) purpose of training sailors for warships, thereby aiding the prosecution of wars in Europe. And all this is the work of powers who make endless ado about their piety, and who wish to be considered as chosen believers while they live on the fruits of iniquity.

The peoples of the earth have thus entered in varying degrees into a universal community, and it has developed to the point where a violation of rights in *one* part of the world is felt *everywhere*. The idea of a cosmopolitan right is therefore not fantastic and overstrained; it is a necessary complement to the unwritten code of political and international right, transforming it into a universal right of humanity. Only under this condition can we flatter ourselves that we are continually advancing towards a perpetual peace.

First Supplement: On the Guarantee of a Perpetual Peace

Perpetual peace is *guaranteed* by no less an authority than the great artist *Nature* herself (*natura daedala rerum* [Nature the contriver of things]). The mechanical process of nature visibly exhibits the purposive plan of producing concord among men, even against their will and indeed by means of their very discord. This design, if we regard it as a compelling cause whose laws of operation are unknown to us, is called *fate*. But if we consider its purposive function within the world's development, whereby it appears as the underlying wisdom of a higher cause, showing the way towards the objective goal of the human race and predetermining the world's evolution,

we call it *providence*.[11] We cannot actually observe such
an agency in the artifices of nature, nor can we even *infer*
its existence from them. But as with all relations between
the form of things and their ultimate purposes, we can
and must *supply it mentally* in order to conceive of its
possibility by analogy with human artifices. Its relationship to and conformity with the end which reason
directly prescribes to us (i.e. the end of morality) can
only be conceived of as an idea. Yet while this idea is
indeed far-fetched in *theory*, it does possess dogmatic
validity and has a very real foundation in *practice*, as with
the concept of *perpetual peace*, which makes it our duty
to promote it by using the natural mechanism described
above. But in contexts such as this, where we are concerned purely with theory and not with religion, we
should also note that it is more in keeping with the
limitations of human reason to speak of *nature* and not
of *providence*, for reason, in dealing with cause and effect
relationships, must keep within the bounds of possible
experience. *Modesty* forbids us to speak of providence
as something we can recognize, for this would mean
donning the wings of Icarus and presuming to approach
the mystery of its inscrutable intentions.

But before we define this guarantee more precisely,
we must first examine the situation in which nature has
placed the actors in her great spectacle, for it is this situation which ultimately demands the guarantee of peace.
We may next inquire in what manner the guarantee
is provided.

Nature's provisional arrangement is as follows. Firstly,
she has taken care that human beings are able to live in

all the areas where they are settled. Secondly, she has driven them in all directions by means of *war*, so that they inhabit even the most inhospitable regions. And thirdly, she has compelled them by the same means to enter into more or less legal relationships. It is in itself wonderful that moss can still grow in the cold wastes around the Arctic Ocean; the *reindeer* can scrape it out from beneath the snow, and can thus itself serve as nourishment or as a draft animal for the Ostiaks or Samoyeds. Similarly, the sandy salt deserts contain the *camel*, which seems as if it had been created for travelling over them in order that they might not be left unutilized. But evidence of design in nature emerges even more clearly when we realize that the shores of the Arctic Ocean are inhabited not only by fur-bearing animals, but also by seals, walruses and whales, whose flesh provides food and whose fat provides warmth for the native inhabitants. Nature's care arouses most admiration, however, by carrying driftwood to these treeless regions, without anyone knowing exactly where it comes from. For if they did not have this material, the natives would not be able to construct either boats or weapons, or dwellings in which to live. And they have enough to do making war on the animals to be able to live in peace among themselves. But it was probably nothing but war which *drove* them into these regions. And the first *instrument of war* among all the animals which man learned to domesticate in the course of peopling the earth was the *horse*. For the elephant belongs to that later age of luxury which began after states had been established. The same applies to the art of cultivating certain kinds of grasses known as *cereals*, whose original nature is now unknown to us, and to the production and refinement of various *fruits* by transplanting and grafting (in Europe, perhaps only two species were involved, the crab-apple and the wild pear). Such arts could arise only within established states in which landed property was secure, after men had made the transition to an *agricultural* way of life, abandoning the lawless freedom they had enjoyed in their previous existence as hunters,[12] fishers and shepherds. *Salt* and *iron* were next discovered, and were perhaps the first articles of trade between nations to be in demand everywhere. In this way, nations first entered into *peaceful relations* with one another, and thus achieved mutual understanding, community of interests and peaceful relations, even with the most distant of their fellows.

In seeing to it that men *could* live everywhere on earth, nature has at the same time despotically willed that they *should* live everywhere, even against their own inclinations. And this obligation does not rest upon any concept of duty which might bind them to fulfil it in accordance with a moral law; on the contrary, nature has chosen war as a means of attaining this end.

We can observe nations which reveal the unity of their descent by the unity of their language. This is the case with the *Samoyeds* on the Arctic Ocean and another people with a similar language living two hundred miles away in the Altai Mountains; another people of Mongol extraction, given to horsemanship and hence to warlike pursuits, has pushed its way between them, thus driving the one part of the tribe far away from the other into the most inhospitable Arctic regions, where it would certainly not have gone by its own inclinations.[13] In the same way, the Finns in the northernmost region of Europe (where they are known as Lapps) are now far separated from the Hungarians, to whom they are linguistically related, by Gothic and Sarmatian peoples who have pushed their way in between them. And what else but war, nature's means of peopling the whole earth, can have driven the Eskimos so far North – for they are quite distinct from all other American races, and are perhaps descended from European adventurers of ancient times; the Pesherae have been driven South into Tierra del Fuego in the same manner. War itself, however, does not require any particular kind of motivation, for it seems to be ingrained in human nature, and even to be regarded as something noble to which man is inspired by his love of honour, without selfish motives. Thus warlike courage, with the American savages as with their European counterparts in medieval times, is held to be of great and immediate value – and not just *in times of* war (as might be expected), but also *in order that* there may be war. Thus wars are often started merely to display this quality, so that war itself is invested with an inherent *dignity*; for even philosophers have eulogized it as a kind of ennobling influence on man, forgetting the Greek saying that 'war is bad in that it produces more evil people than it destroys'. So much, then, for what nature does to further *her own end* with respect to the human race as an animal species.

We now come to the essential question regarding the prospect of perpetual peace. What does nature do in relation to the end which man's own reason prescribes to him as a duty, i.e. how does nature help to promote his *moral purpose*? And how does nature guarantee that what man *ought* to do by the laws of his freedom (but does not do) will in fact be done through nature's compulsion, without prejudice to the free agency of man? This question arises, moreover, in all three areas of public right – in *political, international* and *cosmopolitan right*. For if I say that nature *wills* that this or that should happen, this does not mean that nature imposes on us a *duty* to do it, for duties can only be imposed by practical reason, acting without any external constraint. On the contrary, nature does it herself, whether we are willing or not: *fata volentem ducunt, nolentem trahunt* ['the fates lead him who is willing, but drag him who is unwilling'].

I. Even if people were not compelled by internal dissent to submit to the coercion of public laws, war would produce the same effect from outside. For in accordance with the natural arrangement described above, each people would find itself confronted by another neighbouring people pressing in upon it, thus forcing it to form itself internally into a *state* in order to encounter the other as an armed *power*. Now the *republican* constitution is the only one which does complete justice to the rights of man. But it is also the most difficult to establish, and even more so to preserve, so that many maintain that it would only be possible within a state of *angels*, since men, with their self-seeking inclinations, would be incapable of adhering to a constitution of so sublime a nature. But in fact, nature comes to the aid of the universal and rational human will, so admirable in itself but so impotent in practice, and makes use of precisely those self-seeking inclinations in order to do so. It only remains for men to create a good organization for the state, a task which is well within their capability, and to arrange it in such a way that their self-seeking energies are opposed to one another, each thereby neutralizing or eliminating the destructive effects of the rest. And as far as reason is concerned, the result is the same as if man's selfish tendencies were non-existent, so that man, even if he is not morally good in himself, is nevertheless compelled to be a good citizen. As hard as it may sound, the problem of setting up a state can be solved even by a nation of devils (so long as they possess understanding). It may be stated as follows: 'In order to organize a group of rational beings who together require universal laws for their survival, but of whom each separate individual is secretly inclined to exempt himself from them, the constitution must be so designed that, although the citizens are opposed to one another in their private attitudes, these opposing views may inhibit one another in such a way that the public conduct of the citizens will be the same as if they did not have such evil attitudes.' A problem of this kind must be soluble. For such a task does not involve the moral improvement of man; it only means finding out how the mechanism of nature can be applied to men in such a manner that the antagonism of their hostile attitudes will make them compel one another to submit to coercive laws, thereby producing a condition of peace within which the laws can be enforced. We can even see this principle at work among the actually existing (although as yet very imperfectly organized) states. For in their external relations, they have already approached what the idea of right prescribes, although the reason for this is certainly not their internal moral attitudes. In the same way, we cannot expect their moral attitudes to produce a good political constitution; on the contrary, it is only through the latter that the people can be expected to attain a good level of moral culture. Thus that mechanism of nature by which selfish inclinations are naturally opposed to one another in their external relations can be used by reason to facilitate the attainment of its own end, the reign of established right. Internal and external peace are thereby furthered and assured, so far as it lies within the power of the state itself to do so. We may therefore say that nature *irresistibly wills* that right should eventually gain the upper hand. What men have neglected to do will ultimately happen of its own accord, albeit with much inconvenience. As Bouterwek puts it: 'If the reed is bent too far, it breaks; and he who wants too much gets nothing.'

2. The idea of international right presupposes the separate existence of many independent adjoining states. And such a state of affairs is essentially a state of war, unless there is a federal union to prevent hostilities breaking out. But in the light of the idea of reason, this state is still to be preferred to an amalgamation of the separate nations under a single power which has over-ruled the rest and created a universal monarchy. For the laws progressively lose their impact as the government increases its range, and a soulless despotism, after crushing the germs of goodness, will finally lapse into anarchy.

It is nonetheless the desire of every state (or its ruler) to achieve lasting peace by thus dominating the whole world, if at all possible. But *nature* wills it otherwise, and uses two means to separate the nations and prevent them from intermingling – *linguistic* and *religious*[14] differences. These may certainly occasion mutual hatred and provide pretexts for wars, but as culture grows and men gradually move towards greater agreement over their principles, they lead to mutual understanding and peace. And unlike that universal despotism which saps all man's energies and ends in the graveyard of freedom, this peace is created and guaranteed by an equilibrium of forces and a most vigorous rivalry.

3. Thus nature wisely separates the nations, although the will of each individual state, even basing its arguments on international right, would gladly unite them under its own sway by force or by cunning. On the other hand, nature also unites nations which the concept of cosmopolitan right would not have protected from violence and war, and does so by means of their mutual self-interest. For the *spirit of commerce* sooner or later takes hold of every people, and it cannot exist side by side with war. And of all the powers (or means) at the disposal of the power of the state, *financial power* can probably be relied on most. Thus states find themselves compelled to promote the noble cause of peace, though not exactly from motives of morality. And wherever in the world there is a threat of war breaking out, they will try to prevent it by mediation, just as if they had entered into a permanent league for this purpose; for by the very nature of things, large military alliances can

only rarely be formed, and will even more rarely be successful.

In this way, nature guarantees perpetual peace by the actual mechanism of human inclinations. And while the likelihood of its being attained is not sufficient to enable us to *prophesy* the future theoretically, it is enough for practical purposes. It makes it our duty to work our way towards this goal, which is more than an empty chimera.

Second Supplement: Secret Article of a Perpetual Peace

In transactions involving public right, a secret article (regarded objectively or in terms of its content) is a contradiction. But in subjective terms, i.e. in relation to the sort of person who dictates it, an article may well contain a secret element, for the person concerned may consider it prejudicial to his own dignity to name himself publicly as its originator.

The only article of this kind is embodied in the following sentence: *'The maxims of the philosophers on the conditions under which public peace is possible shall be consulted by states which are armed for war.'*

Although it may seem humiliating for the legislative authority of a state, to which we must naturally attribute the highest degree of wisdom, to seek instruction from *subjects* (the philosophers) regarding the principles on which it should act in its relations with other states, it is nevertheless extremely advisable that it should do so. The state will therefore invite their help *silently*, making a secret of it. In other words, it will *allow them to speak* freely and publicly on the universal maxims of warfare and peace-making, and they will indeed do so of their own accord if no one forbids their discussions. And no special formal arrangement among the states is necessary to enable them to agree on this issue, for the agreement already lies in the obligations imposed by universal human reason in its capacity as a moral legislator. This does not, however, imply that the state must give the principles of the philosopher precedence over the pronouncements of the jurist (who represents the power of the state), but only that the philosopher should be given a *hearing*. The jurist, who has taken as his symbol the scales of right and the sword of justice, usually uses the latter not merely to keep any extraneous influences away from the former, but will throw the *sword* into one of the *scales* if it refuses to sink (*vae victis!*). Unless the jurist is at the same time a philosopher, at any rate in moral matters, he is under the greatest temptation to do this, for his business is merely to apply existing laws, and not to inquire whether they are in need of improvement. He acts as if this truly low rank of his faculty were in fact one of the higher ones, for the simple reason that it is accompanied by power (as is also the case with two of the other faculties). But the philosophical faculty occupies a very low position in face of the combined power of the others. Thus we are told, for instance, that philosophy is the *handmaid* of theology, and something similar in relation to the others. But it is far from clear whether this handmaid bears the torch before her gracious lady, or carries the train behind.

It is not to be expected that kings will philosophize or that philosophers will become kings; nor is it to be desired, however, since the possession of power inevitably corrupts the free judgement of reason. Kings or sovereign peoples (i.e. those governing themselves by egalitarian laws) should not, however, force the class of philosophers to disappear or to remain silent, but should allow them to speak publicly. This is essential to both in order that light may be thrown on their affairs. And since the class of philosophers is by nature incapable of forming seditious factions or clubs, they cannot incur suspicion of disseminating propaganda.

Appendix

I
On the Disagreement between Morals and Politics in Relation to Perpetual Peace

Morality, as a collection of absolutely binding laws by which our actions *ought* to be governed, belongs essentially, in an objective sense, to the practical sphere. And if we have once acknowledged the authority of this concept of duty, it is patently absurd to say that we *cannot* act as the moral laws require. For if this were the case, the concept of duty would automatically be dropped from morals (*ultra posse nemo obligatur* [no one is obliged to do anything he is incapable of doing]). Hence there can be no conflict between politics, as an applied branch of right, and morality, as a theoretical branch of right (i.e. between theory and practice); for such a conflict could occur only if morality were taken to mean a general doctrine of expediency, i.e. a theory of the maxims by which one might select the most useful means of furthering one's own advantage – and this would be tantamount to denying that morality exists.

If politics were to say: *'Be ye therefore wise as serpents'*, morality might add, by way of qualification: *'and harmless as doves'*. If these two precepts cannot exist together within a single commandment, then there is indeed a disagreement between politics and morality. But if the two are to be united, it is absurd to suppose that they are in opposition, and the question of how such a conflict could be resolved cannot even be posed as a mental exercise. It is true, alas, that the saying *'Honesty is the best policy'* embodies a theory which is frequently contradicted by practice. Yet the equally theoretical proposition *'Honesty is better than any policy'* infinitely transcends all objections, and it is indeed an indispensable condition of any policy whatsoever. The god of morality does not yield to Jupiter, the custodian of violence, for even Jupiter is still subject to fate. In short, reason is not sufficiently enlightened to discover the whole series of predetermining causes which would allow it to predict accurately the happy or unhappy consequences of human activities as dictated by the mechanism of nature; it can only hope that the result will meet with its wishes. But reason at all times shows us clearly enough what we have to do in order to remain on the paths of duty, as the rules of wisdom require, and thus shows us the way towards our ultimate goal.

But the man of practice, to whom morality is pure theory, coldly repudiates our well-intentioned hopes, even if he does concede that we *can* do what we *ought* to do. He bases his argument on the claim that we can tell in advance from human nature that man will never *want* to do what is necessary in order to attain the goal of eternal peace. It is perfectly true that the will of all *individual* men to live in accordance with principles of freedom within a lawful constitution (i.e. the *distributive* unity of the will of all) is not sufficient for this purpose. Before so difficult a problem can be solved, all men *together* (i.e. the *collective* unity of the combined will) must desire to attain this goal; only then can civil society exist as a single whole. Since an additional unifying cause must therefore overrule the differences in the particular wishes of all individuals before a common will can arise, and since no single individual can create it, the only conceivable way of executing the original idea *in practice*, and hence of inaugurating a state of right, is by *force*. On its coercive authority, public right will subsequently be based.

We can certainly expect in advance that there will be considerable deviations in actual experience from the original theoretical idea. For we cannot assume that the moral attitude of the legislator will be such that, after the disorderly mass has been united into a people, he will leave them to create a lawful constitution by their own common will.

It might thus be said that, once a person has the power in his own hands, he will not let the people prescribe laws for him. Similarly, a state which is self-governing and free from all external laws will not let itself become dependent on the judgement of other states in seeking to uphold its rights against them. And even a whole continent, if it feels itself in a superior position to another one, will not hesitate to plunder it or actually to extend its rule over it, irrespective of whether the other is in its way or not. In this way, all the plans which theory lays for political, international or cosmopolitan right dissolve into empty and impracticable ideals; but a practice which is based on empirical principles of human nature, and which does not consider it beneath its dignity to shape its maxims according to the way of the world, can alone hope to find a solid foundation for its system of political opportunism.

If, of course, there is neither freedom nor any moral law based on freedom, but only a state in which everything that happens or can happen simply obeys the mechanical workings of nature, politics would mean the art of utilizing nature for the government of men, and this would constitute the whole of practical wisdom; the concept of right would then be only an empty idea. But if we consider it absolutely necessary to couple the concept of right with politics, or even to make it a limiting condition of politics, it must be conceded that the two are compatible. And I can indeed imagine a *moral politician*, i.e. someone who conceives of the principles of political expediency in such a way that they can co-exist with morality, but I cannot imagine a *political moralist*, i.e. one who fashions his morality to suit his own advantage as a statesman.

The moral politician will make it a principle that, if any faults which could not have been prevented are discovered in the political constitution or in the relations between states, it is a duty, especially for heads of state, to see to it that they are corrected as soon as possible; it should be ensured that these political institutions are made to conform to natural right, which stands before us as a model in the idea of practical reason, and this should be done even if selfish interests have to be sacrificed. It would be contrary to all political expediency, which in this case agrees with morality, to destroy any of the existing bonds of political or cosmopolitan union before a better constitution has been prepared to take their place. And while it would be absurd to demand that their faults be repaired at once and by violent measures, it can still be required of the individual in power that he should be intimately aware of the maxim that changes for the better are necessary, in order that the constitution may constantly approach the optimum end prescribed by laws of right. A state may well *govern* itself in a republican way, even if its existing constitution provides for a despotic *ruling power*; and it will gradually come to the stage where the people can be influenced by the mere idea of the law's authority, just as if it were backed up by physical force, so that they will be able to create for themselves a legislation ultimately founded on right. If, however, a more lawful constitution were attained by unlawful means, i.e. by a violent *revolution* resulting from a previous bad constitution, it would then no longer be permissible to lead the people back to the original one, even although everyone who had interfered with the old constitution by violence or conspiracy would rightly have been subject to the penalties of rebellion during the revolution itself. But as for the external relationship between states, no state can be required to relinquish its constitution, even if the latter is despotic (and hence stronger in relation to external enemies), so long as this state is in danger of being engulfed at any moment by other states; hence while plans must be made for political improvement, it must be permissible to delay their execution until a better opportunity arises.[15]

It may well be the case that despotic moralists, i.e. those who err in practice, frequently act contrary to political prudence by adopting or recommending premature measures, yet experience must gradually bring them out of their opposition to nature and make them adopt better ways. But moralizing politicians, for what they are worth, try to cover up political principles which are contrary to right, under the pretext that human nature is *incapable* of attaining the good which reason prescribes as an idea. They thereby make progress *impossible*, and eternalize the violation of right.

Instead of applying the correct practice they boast of, these worldly-wise politicians resort to despicable tricks, for they are only out to exploit the people (and if possible the whole world) by influencing the current ruling power in such a way as to ensure their own private advantage. They are just like lawyers (i.e. those for whom law is a profession, not a matter of legislation) who have found their way into politics. For since it is not their business to argue over legislation itself, but to fulfil the present instructions of the law of the land, they will always regard the existing legal constitution (or, if this is altered by a higher authority, the subsequent one) as the best, because everything in it will follow a proper mechanical order. But this skill in being all things to all men may give them the illusion that they can also pass judgement, in accordance with concepts of right (i.e. *a priori*, not empirically), on the principles of any *political constitution* whatsoever. And they may boast that they know *men* (which is certainly to be expected, since they have to do with so many of them), although they do not know *man* and his potentialities, for this requires a higher anthropological vantage-point.

Armed with concepts such as these, they proceed to take up political and international law as prescribed by reason. But they cannot take this step except in a spirit of chicanery, for they will follow their usual procedure of applying despotically formulated coercive laws in a mechanical manner, even in a sphere where the concepts of reason only allow for lawful coercion, in keeping with the principles of freedom, which alone make possible a rightfully established political constitution. The supposed practitioner believes he can solve this problem empirically, ignoring the idea of reason and drawing on experience of how the (largely unlawful) constitutions which have hitherto survived best were organized. And the maxims which he employs for this purpose, although he does not make them public, can roughly be expressed in the following sophistries:

1. *Fac et excusa* [Act first and justify your actions later]. Seize any favourable opportunity of arbitrarily expropriating a right which the state enjoys over its own or over a neighbouring people; the justification can be presented far more easily and elegantly and the use of violence can be glossed over far more readily *after the fact* than if one were to think out convincing reasons in advance and then wait for counter-arguments to be offered. This is particularly true of the first case, where the highest power in the state is also the legislative authority which must be obeyed without argument. Such audacity itself gives a certain appearance of inner conviction that the deed is right and just, and the god of

success (*bonus eventus*) will then be the best of advocates.

2. *Si fecisti, nega* [If you are the perpetrator, deny it]. If you have committed a crime, for instance, in order to lead your people to desperation and thence to rebellion, deny that the guilt is yours. Maintain instead that it arose from the intransigence of the subjects; or if you have seized control of a neighbouring people, say that the very nature of man is responsible, for if he does not anticipate others in resorting to violence, he may count on it that they will anticipate and overpower him.

3. *Divide et impera* [Divide and rule]. That is, if there are certain privileged persons among the people who have chosen you for their ruler merely as *primus inter pares* [the chief among his peers], make sure to disunite them among themselves and set them at odds with the people. And if you back up the people with false promises of greater freedom, everything will be dependent on your absolute will. Or if you are dealing with foreign states, to stir up discord among them is a fairly certain method of subjugating them one by one while merely appearing to lend support to the weaker.

No one, it must be confessed, will be taken in by these political maxims, for they are all generally known. And it is not the case that men are ashamed of them, as if their injustice were all too obviously visible. For great powers are never embarrassed about how the common mass might judge them, but only about one another's opinions. And as for the principles listed above, the powers will feel no shame if they become publicly known, but only if they *fail to succeed*, for they are all agreed on the moral status of the maxims. They are left with *political honour*, on which they can always rely if they *enlarge their power* by whatever means they care to use.[16] From all these twists and turns of an immoral and opportunistic doctrine of how to create peace among men out of the warlike state of nature, this much at least is clear: men can as little escape the concept of right in their private relations as in their public ones, and they will not openly dare to base their politics on opportunistic machinations alone and thus to refuse altogether to obey any concept of public right (which is particularly remarkable in the case of international right). Instead, they pay such concepts all the honour they deserve, even although they may also devise a hundred excuses and subterfuges to get out of observing them in practice and to pretend that brute force and cunning can possess that authority which is the source and unifying bond of all right.

In order to end this sophistry (if not the actual injustice which it covers over) and to make the false representatives of those who wield power on earth confess that they are advocating might instead of right (adopting as they do the tone of persons entitled to give orders), it will be well to discover the ultimate principle from which the end of perpetual peace is derived, and thus to destroy the illusions with which men deceive themselves and others. It must likewise be demonstrated that all the evil which stands in the way of perpetual peace results from the fact that the political moralist starts out from the very point at which the moral politician rightly stops; he thus makes his principles subordinate to his end (i.e. puts the cart before the horse), thereby defeating his own purpose of reconciling politics with morality.

To ensure that practical philosophy is at one with itself, it is first necessary to resolve the question of whether, in problems of practical reason, we should begin with its *material* principle, i.e. its *end*, as an object of the will, or with its *formal* principle, i.e. the principle which rests on man's freedom in his external relations and which states: 'Act in such a way that you can wish your maxim to become a universal law (irrespective of what the end in view may be).'

The latter principle must undoubtedly take precedence. For as a principle of right, it has absolute necessity, whereas the former is necessary only if the empirical conditions which permit the proposed end to be realized can be assumed to exist. And if this end were also a duty, as with the end of perpetual peace, it would itself have to be deduced from the formal principle of the maxims governing external action. Now the former (i.e. material) principle is that of the *political moralist*, and it treats the problems of political, international and cosmopolitan right as mere *technical tasks*; but the latter (i.e. formal) principle is that of the *moral politician*, for whom it is a *moral task*, totally different in its execution from technical problems, to bring about perpetual peace, which is desirable not just as a physical good, but also as a state of affairs which must arise out of recognizing one's duty.

For the solution of the first problem (that of political expediency), much knowledge of nature is required, so that one can use its mechanism to promote the intended end. Nevertheless, all this is uncertain so far as its repercussions on perpetual peace are concerned, no matter which of the three departments of public right one considers. For it is uncertain whether the obedience and prosperity of the people can be better maintained over a long period by strict discipline or by appeals to their vanity, by conferring supreme power upon a single individual or upon several united leaders, or perhaps merely by means of an aristocracy of office or by popular internal government. History offers examples of the opposite effect being produced by all forms of government, with the single exception of genuine republicanism, which, however, could be the object only of a moral politician. And it is even more uncertain in the case of an *international right* supposedly based on statutes worked out by ministers, for it is in fact a mere word with nothing behind it, since it depends upon treaties which contain in the very act of their conclusion the secret reservation that they may be violated. On the other hand, the solution of the second problem, that of *political wisdom*, presents itself as it were automatically; it is obvious to everyone, it defeats all artifices, and leads straight to its goal, so long as we prudently remember that it cannot be realized by violent and precipitate means, but must be steadily approached as favourable opportunities present themselves.

We may therefore offer the following advice: 'Seek ye first the kingdom of pure practical reason and its *righteousness*, and your object (the blessing of perpetual peace) will be added unto you.' For morality, with regard to its principles of public right (hence in relation to a political code which can be known *a priori*), has the peculiar feature that the less it makes its conduct depend upon the end it envisages (whether this be a physical or moral advantage), the more it will in general harmonize with this end. And the reason for this is that it is precisely the general will as it is given *a priori*, within a single people or in the mutual relationships of various peoples, which alone determines what is right among men. But this union of the will of all, if only it is put into practice in a consistent way, can also, within the mechanism of nature, be the cause which leads to the intended result and gives effect to the concept of right. For example, it is a principle of moral politics that a people should combine to form a state in accordance with freedom and equality as its sole concepts of right, and this principle is based not on expediency, but on duty. Political moralists, on the other hand, do not deserve a hearing, however much they argue about the natural mechanism of a mass of people who enter into society, or claim that this mechanism would invalidate the above principles and frustrate their fulfilment, or try to prove their assertions by citing examples of badly organized constitutions of ancient and modern times (e.g. of democracies without a system of representation). Such theories are particularly damaging, because they may themselves produce the very evil they predict. For they put man into the same class as other living machines, which only need to realize consciously that they are not free beings for them to become in their own eyes the most wretched of all earthly creatures.

The proverbial saying *fiat iustitia, pereat mundus* (i.e. let justice reign, even if all the rogues in the world must perish) may sound somewhat inflated, but it is nonetheless true. It is a sound principle of right, which blocks up all the devious paths followed by cunning or violence. But it must not be misunderstood, or taken, for example, as a permit to apply one's own rights with the utmost rigour (which would conflict with ethical duty), but should be seen as an obligation of those in power not to deny or detract from the rights of anyone out of disfavour or sympathy for others. And this requires above all that the state should have an internal constitution organized in accordance with pure principles of right, and also that it unite with other neighbouring or even distant states to arrive at a lawful settlement of their differences by forming something analogous to a universal state. This proposition simply means that whatever the physical consequences may be, the political maxims adopted must not be influenced by the prospect of any benefit or happiness which might accrue to the state if it followed them, i.e. by the end which each state takes as the object of its will (as the highest *empirical* principle of political wisdom); they should be influenced only by the pure concept of rightful duty, i.e. by an obligation whose principle is given *a priori* by pure reason. The world will certainly not come to an end if there are fewer bad men. Moral evil has by nature the inherent quality of being self-destructive and self-contradictory in its aims (especially in relations between persons of a like mind), so that it makes way for the moral principle of goodness, even if such progress is slow.

Thus in *objective* or theoretical terms, there is no conflict whatsoever between morality and politics. In a *subjective* sense, however (i.e. in relation to the selfish disposition of man, which, since it is not based on maxims of reason, cannot however be called practice), this conflict will and ought to remain active, since it serves as a whetstone of virtue. The true courage of virtue, according to the principle *tu ne cede malis, sed contra audentior ito* ['You for your part must not give way to troubles, but confront them the more boldly'], does not so much consist, in the present case, in resolutely standing up to the evils and sacrifices which must be encountered, as in facing the evil principle within ourselves and overcoming its wiles. For this principle is far more dangerous, since it is deceitful, treacherous, and liable to exploit the weakness of human nature in order to justify any violation of justice.

The political moralist may indeed say that the ruler and people, or one people and another people, do no injustice to *each other* if they enter into mutual conflict through violence or cunning, although they act completely unjustly in refusing to respect the concept of right, which would alone be capable of establishing perpetual peace. For if one party violates his duty towards another who is just as lawlessly disposed towards him, that which actually *happens* to them in wearing each other out is perfectly just, and enough of their kind will always survive to keep this process going without interruption into the most distant future, so that later generations may take them as a warning example. Providence is justified in disposing the course of world events in this way; for the moral principle in man is never extinguished, and reason, which is pragmatically capable of applying the ideas of right according to this principle, constantly increases with the continuous progress of culture, while the guilt attending violations of right increases proportionately. If we suppose that mankind never can or will be in a better condition, it seems impossible to justify by any kind of theodicy the mere fact that such a race of corrupt beings could have been created on earth at all. But this kind of judgement is far too exalted for us; we cannot theoretically attribute our conception of wisdom to the supreme power whose nature is beyond our understanding.

Such are the desperate conclusions to which we are inevitably driven if we do not assume that the pure principles of right have an objective reality, i.e. that they can be applied in practice. And whatever empirical politics may say to the contrary, the people within the state, as well as the states in their relations with one another, must act accordingly. A true system of politics cannot therefore take a single step without first paying tribute to morality. And although politics in itself is a difficult art, no art is required to combine it with morality. For as soon as the two come into conflict, morality can cut through the knot which politics cannot untie.

The rights of man must be held sacred, however great a sacrifice the ruling power may have to make. There can be no half measures here; it is no use devising hybrid solutions such as a pragmatically conditioned right halfway between right and utility. For all politics must bend the knee before right, although politics may hope in return to arrive, however slowly, at a stage of lasting brilliance.

II
On the Agreement Between Politics and Morality According to the Transcendental Concept of Public Right

If, in considering public right as the jurists usually conceive of it, I abstract from all its *material* aspects (as determined by the various empirically given relationships of men within a state, or of states with one another), I am left with the *formal attribute of publicness*. For every claim upon right potentially possesses this attribute, and without it, there can be no justice (which can only be conceived of as *publicly knowable*) and therefore no right, since right can only come from justice.

Every claim upon right must have this public quality, and since it is very easy to judge whether or not it is present in a particular instance, i.e. whether or not it can be combined with the principles of the agent concerned, it provides us with a readily applicable criterion which can be discovered *a priori* within reason itself. If it cannot be reconciled with the agent's principles, it enables us to recognize at once the falseness (i.e. unrightfulness) of the claim (*praetensio iuris*) in question, as if by an experiment of pure reason.

After we have abstracted in this way from all the empirical elements contained within the concept of political and international right (including that evil aspect of human nature which makes coercion necessary), we may specify the following proposition as the *transcendental formula* of public right: 'All actions affecting the rights of other human beings are wrong if their maxim is not compatible with their being made public.'

This principle should be regarded not only as *ethical* (i.e. pertaining to the theory of virtue) but also as *juridical* (i.e. affecting the rights of man). For a maxim which I may not *declare openly* without thereby frustrating my own intention, or which must at all costs be *kept secret* if it is to succeed, or which I cannot *publicly acknowledge* without thereby inevitably arousing the resistance of everyone to my plans, can only have stirred up this necessary and general (hence *a priori* foreseeable) opposition against me because it is itself unjust and thus constitutes a threat to everyone. Besides, this is a purely *negative* test, i.e. it serves only as a means of detecting what is *not* right in relation to others. Like any axiom, it is valid without demonstration, and besides, it is easy to apply, as can be seen from the following examples of public right.

1. In the *internal right of a state* (*ius civitatis*), a question may arise which many people consider difficult to answer, although it can be resolved quite easily by means of the transcendental principle of publicness. It runs as follows: 'Is rebellion a rightful means for a people to use in order to overthrow the oppressive power of a so-called tyrant (*non titulo, sed exercitio talis*)?' The rights of the people have been violated, and there can be no doubt that the tyrant would not be receiving unjust treatment if he were dethroned. Nevertheless, it is in the highest degree wrong if the subjects pursue their rights in this way, and they cannot in the least complain of injustice if they are defeated in the ensuing conflict and subsequently have to endure the most severe penalties.

Much can be said in arguments both for and against such a course of action if we try to settle the matter by dogmatic deduction of the principles of right. But the transcendental principle of publicness in questions of right can get round such long-winded discussion. According to this principle, the people, before establishing the civil contract, asks itself whether it dares to make public the maxim of its intention to rebel on certain occasions. It is easily seen that if one were to make it a condition of founding a political constitution that force might in certain eventualities be used against the head of state, the people would have to claim rightful authority over its ruler. But if this were so, the ruler would not be the head of state; or if *both* parties were given authority as a prior condition of establishing the state, the existence of the state itself, which it was the people's intention to establish, would become impossible. The injustice of rebellion is thus apparent from the fact that if the maxim upon which it would act *were publicly acknowledged*, it would defeat its own purpose. This maxim would therefore have to be kept secret.

But it would not be necessary for the head of state to conceal his intentions. He may say quite openly that he will punish any rebellion by putting the ringleaders to death, even if they believed that he was himself the first to infringe the fundamental law. For if he is aware that he possesses *irresistible* supreme power (and this must be assumed in any civil constitution, for a ruler who does not have sufficient power to protect each individual among the people against the others cannot have the right to give the people orders either), he does not have to worry that his own aims might be frustrated if his maxim became generally known. And it is perfectly consistent with this argument that if the people were to rebel successfully, the head of state would revert to the position of a subject; but he would not be justified in starting a new rebellion to restore his former position, nor should he have to fear being called to account for his previous administration.

2. We now come to *international right*. – We can speak of international right only on the assumption that some kind of lawful condition exists, i.e. that external circumstances are such that a man can genuinely be accorded his rights. For as a form of public right, it implies by definition that there is a general will which publicly assigns to each individual that which is his due. And this *status iuridicus* must be derived from some sort of contract, which, unlike that from which a state originates, must not be based on coercive laws, but may at most be a state of *permanent and free association* like the above-mentioned federation of different states. For without some kind of *lawful condition* which actively links together the various physical or moral persons (as is the case in the state of nature), the only possible form of right is a private one. This again involves a conflict between politics and morality (the latter in the shape of a theory of right). The criterion of publicness in the relevant maxims can, however, once again be easily applied, but only on condition that the contract binds the states for the single purpose of preserving peace amongst themselves and in relation to other states, and on no account with a view to military conquest. We can

thus envisage the following instances of an antinomy between politics and morality, along with the appropriate solution in each case.

(*a*) 'If one of these states has promised something to another, whether it be assistance, cession of certain territories, subsidies, or the like, it may be asked whether this state, on occasions when its own welfare is at stake, may free itself from the obligation to keep its word, maintaining that it ought to be regarded as a dual person – on the one hand, as a *sovereign* who is not responsible to anyone within the state, and on the other, merely as the highest political *official* who is responsible to the state; and the conclusion to be drawn from this is that the state (or its ruler) can be exempted in the latter capacity from obligations it incurred in the first.' But if the ruler of a state were to let it be known that this was his maxim, everyone else would naturally flee from him, or unite with others in order to resist his pretensions; which proves that such a system of politics, for all its cunning, would defeat its own purpose if it operated on a public footing, so that the above maxim must be wrong.

(*b*) 'If a neighbouring power which has grown to a formidable size (*potentia tremenda*) gives cause for anxiety, can one assume that it will *wish* to oppress other states because is *is able* to do so, and does this give the less powerful party a right to mount a concerted attack upon it, even if no offence has been offered?' If a state were to *let it be known* that it affirmed this maxim, it would merely bring about more surely and more quickly the very evil it feared. For the greater power would anticipate the lesser ones, and the possibility that they might unite would be but a feeble reed against one who knew how to use the tactics of *divide et impera*. Thus this maxim of political expediency, if acknowledged publicly, necessarily defeats its own purpose and is consequently unjust.

(*c*) 'If a smaller state, by its geographical situation, constitutes a gap in the territory of a larger state, and this larger state requires the intrusive territory for its own preservation, is not the larger state justified in subjugating the smaller one and in annexing its territory?' One can easily see that the larger state must on no account let it be known that it has adopted such a maxim. For the smaller states would either unite in good time, or other powerful states would quarrel over the proposed prey, so that the plan would be rendered impracticable if it were made public. This is a sign that it is unjust, and it would in fact be an injustice of very great magnitude; for the fact that the object of an injustice is small does not mean that the injustice done to it may not be very great.

3. As for *cosmopolitan right*, I pass over it here in silence, for its maxims are easy to formulate and assess on account of its analogy with international right.

In the principle that the maxims of international right may be incompatible with publicity, we thus have a good indication that politics and morality (in the sense of a theory of right) are *not in agreement*. But it is also necessary that we should know what the condition is under which its maxims will agree with international right. For we cannot simply conclude by a reverse process that all maxims which can be made public are therefore also just, because the person who has decisive supremacy has no need to conceal his maxims. The condition which must be fulfilled before any kind of international right is possible is that a *lawful state* must already be in existence. For without this, there can be no public right, and any right which can be conceived of outside it, i.e. in a state of nature, will be merely a private right. Now we have already seen above that a federative association of states whose sole intention is to eliminate war is the only *lawful* arrangement which can be reconciled with their *freedom*. Thus politics and morality can only be in agreement within a federal union, which is therefore necessary and given *a priori* through the principles of right. And the rightful basis of all political prudence is the founding of such a union in the most comprehensive form possible; for without this aim, all its reasonings are unwisdom and veiled injustice. This kind of false politics has its own *casuistry* to match that of the best Jesuit scholars. For it includes the *reservatio mentalis* whereby public contracts are formulated in terms which one can interpret to one's own advantage as required (for example, the distinction between the *status quo* of fact and the *status quo* of right); it also includes the *probabilismus*, i.e. it tries to think out evil intentions which it might attribute to others, or uses the likelihood of their gaining predominance as a legal justification for undermining other peaceful states; and finally, it has the principle of the philosophical sin (*peccatum philosophicum*, *peccatillum*, or *bagatelle*), whereby it can be regarded as a readily pardonable trifle to seize a *small* state if a much *larger* state gains in the process, to the supposed advantage of the world in general.[17]

All this is occasioned by the duplicity of politics in relation to morality, for it makes use of whatever branch of morality suits its purposes. But *both* aspects, philanthropy and respect for the *rights* of man, are obligatory. And while the former is only a *conditional* duty, the latter is an *unconditional* and absolutely imperative one; anyone must first be completely sure that he has not infringed it if he wishes to enjoy the sweet sense of having acted justly. Politics can easily be reconciled with morality in the former sense (i.e. as ethics), for both demand that men should give up their rights to their rulers. But when it comes to morality in its second sense (i.e. as the theory of right), which requires that politics should actively defer to it, politics finds it advisable not to enter into any contract at all, preferring to deny that the theory of right has any reality and to reduce all duties to mere acts of goodwill. This subterfuge of a secretive system of politics could, however, easily be defeated if philosophy were to make its maxims public, would it but dare to allow the philosopher to publicize his own maxims.

With this in mind, I now put forward another transcendental and affirmative principle of public right. It might be formulated as follows: 'All maxims which *require* publicity if they are not to fail in their purpose can be reconciled both with right and with politics.'

For if they can only attain their end by being publicized, they must conform to the universal aim of the public (which is happiness), and it is the particular task of politics to remain in harmony with the aim of the public through making it satisfied with its condition. But if this end is to be attained *only* through publicity (i.e. by dispelling all distrust of the maxims employed), the maxims in question must also be in harmony with public right; for only within this right is it possible to unite the ends of everyone. I must, however, postpone the further elaboration and discussion of this principle until another occasion, although it can already be seen that it is a transcendental formula if one removes all the empirical conditions relating to happiness, i.e. the substance of the law, and looks exclusively to the form of universal lawfulness.

If it is a duty to bring about in reality a state of public right (albeit by an infinite process of gradual approximation), and if there are also good grounds for hoping that we shall succeed, then it is not just an empty idea that *perpetual peace* will eventually replace what have hitherto been wrongly called peace treaties (which are actually only truces). On the contrary, it is a task which, as solutions are gradually found, constantly draws nearer fulfilment, for we may hope that the periods within which equal amounts of progress are made will become progressively shorter.

A Renewed Attempt to Answer the Question: 'Is the Human Race Continually Improving?'

1
What Sort of Knowledge are we Looking For?

What we are seeking to know is a portion of human history. It is not a history of the past, however, but a history of future times, i.e. a *predictive* history. But if it is not discoverable from known laws of nature (as with eclipses of the sun and moon, which can be foretold by natural means) and can only be learnt through additional insight into the future supplied by supernatural revelation, it must be termed *prognosticative* or *prophetic*.[18] Besides, we are here concerned not with the natural history of mankind (as we should be if we asked, for example, whether new races of man might emerge in future times), but with the *history of civilization*. And we are not dealing with any *specific* conception of mankind (*singulorum*), but with the *whole* of humanity (*universorum*), united in earthly society and distributed in national groups. All this is implied if we ask whether the human *race* (as a whole) is continually improving.

2
How can we Attain Such Knowledge?

We can obtain a prophetic historical narrative of things to come by depicting those events whose *a priori* possibility suggests that they will in fact happen. But how is it possible to have history *a priori*? The answer is that it is possible if the prophet himself occasions and *produces* the events he predicts.

It was all very well for the Jewish prophets to foretell that the state to which they belonged would sooner or later suffer not only decline, but also complete dissolution; for they were themselves the architects of their fate. As leaders of the people, they had loaded their constitution with so many ecclesiastical (and thence also civil) burdens that their state became completely unfit to exist in its own right, particularly in its relations with neighbouring nations. Thus the jeremiads of the priests naturally went unheeded, because these same priests stubbornly stuck to their belief in the untenable constitution they had themselves created, so that they were themselves able to foresee the consequences with infallible certainty.

Our politicians, so far as their influence extends, behave in exactly the same way, and they are just as successful in their prophecies. One must take men as they are, they tell us, and not as the world's uninformed pedants or good-natured dreamers fancy that they ought to be. But 'as they are' ought to read 'as we have *made them* by unjust coercion, by treacherous designs which the government is in a good position to carry out'. For that is why they are intransigent and inclined to rebellion, and why regrettable consequences ensue if discipline is relaxed in the slightest. In this way, the prophecy of the supposedly clever statesmen is fulfilled.

Various divines also at times prophesy the complete decline of religion and the imminent appearance of the Antichrist, all the while doing the very things that are best calculated to create the state of affairs they describe. For they are not taking care to impress on the hearts of their congregation moral principles which would directly lead to an improvement. Instead, they see observances and historical beliefs as the essential duties, supposing that these will indirectly produce the same results; but although they may lead to mechanical conformity (as within a civil constitution), they cannot produce conformity in moral attitudes. Nevertheless, these divines complain at the irreligion which they have themselves created, and which they could accordingly have foretold without any special gift of prophecy.

3
Subdivisions Within the Concept of what we Wish to Know of the Future

There are three possible forms which our prophecy might take. The human race is either continually *regressing* and deteriorating, continually *progressing* and improving, or at a permanent *standstill*, in relation to other created beings, at its present level of moral attainment (which is the same as continually revolving in a circle around a fixed point).

The first statement might be designated *moral terrorism*, the second *eudaemonism* (which, if the goal of human progress were already visible from afar, might also be termed *chiliasm*), while the third could be called *abderitism*. For in the latter case, since a genuine standstill is impossible in moral affairs, rises and falls of equal magnitude constantly alternate, in endless fluctuation, and produce no more effect than if the subject of them had remained stationary in one place.

a
The terroristic conception of human history

A process of deterioration in the human race cannot go on indefinitely, for mankind would wear itself out after a certain point had been reached. Consequently, when enormities go on piling up and up and the evils they produce continue to increase, we say: 'It can't get much worse now.' It seems that the day of judgement is at hand, and the pious zealot already dreams of the rebirth of everything and of a world created anew after the present world has been destroyed by fire.

b
The eudaemonistic conception of human history

We may readily agree that the sum total of good and evil of which our nature is capable always remains unchanged, and can neither be augmented nor reduced within any one individual. And how could the quantity of good of which a person is capable possibly be increased? For it would have to be done by his own free agency as a subject, and before he could do it, he would in turn require a greater store of goodness than he already possessed in the first place. After all, no effects can exceed the capacity of their effective cause; and the quantity of goodness in man must therefore remain below a certain level in proportion to the amount of evil with which it is intermixed, so that man cannot work his way beyond a given limit and go on improving further. Thus eudaemonism, with its sanguine hopes, appears to be untenable. Its ideas of constant human progress and improvement would seem of little use to a prophetic history of mankind.

c

The hypothesis of abderitism in the human race as a definition of its future history

This point of view probably has the majority of sub-scribers on its side. To start off swiftly along the way of goodness without persevering on it, and instead, to reverse the plan of progress in order at all costs to avoid being tied to a single aim (even if only from a desire for variety); to construct in order to demolish; to take upon ourselves the hopeless task of rolling the stone of Sisyphus uphill, only to let it roll back down again: such is the industrious folly which characterizes our race. In view of all this, it does not so much seem that the principle of evil within the natural character of mankind is amalgamated or fused with that of goodness, but rather that the one is neutralized by the other, with inactivity as the result (or a standstill, as in the case under discussion). This empty activity of backward and forward motion, with good and evil continually alternating, would mean that all the interplay of members of our species on earth ought merely to be regarded as a farce. And in the eyes of reason, this cannot give any higher a value to mankind than to the other animal species, whose interaction takes place at less cost and without any conscious understanding.

4
The Problem of Progress Cannot be Solved Directly from Experience

Even if it were found that the human race as a whole had been moving forward and progressing for an indefinitely long time, no one could guarantee that its era of decline was not beginning at that very moment, by virtue of the physical character of our race. And conversely, if it is regressing and deteriorating at an accelerating pace, there are no grounds for giving up hope that we are just about to reach the turning point (*punctum flexus contrarii*) at which our affairs will take a turn for the better, by virtue of the moral character of our race. For we are dealing with freely acting beings to whom one can *dictate* in advance what they *ought* to do, but of whom one cannot *predict* what they actually *will* do, and who are capable, if things go really badly and they experience evils incurred

72

through their own actions, of regarding these evils as a greater incentive to do better than they did in the past. But as the Abbé Coyer says: 'Poor mortals! Nothing is constant among you but inconstancy.'

Perhaps it is because we have chosen the wrong point of view from which to contemplate the course of human affairs that the latter seems so absurd to us. The planets, as seen from the earth, sometimes move backward, sometimes forward, and at other times remain motionless. But seen from the sun – the point of view of reason – they continually follow their regular paths as in the Copernican hypothesis. Yet some thinkers, otherwise not deficient in wisdom, prefer to stick firmly to their own interpretation of phenomena and to the point of view they originally adopted, even at the price of involving themselves to an absurd degree in Tychonic cycles and epicycles. It is our misfortune, however, that we are unable to adopt an absolute point of view when trying to predict free actions. For this, exalted above all human wisdom, would be the point of view of *providence*, which extends even to *free* human actions. And although man may *see* the latter, he cannot *foresee* them with certainty (a distinction which does not exist in the eyes of the divinity); for while he needs to perceive a connection governed by natural laws before he can foresee anything, he must do without such hints or guidance when dealing with *free* actions in the future.

If it were possible to credit human beings with even a limited will of innate and unvarying goodness, we could certainly predict a general improvement of mankind, for this would involve events which man could himself control. But if man's natural endowments consist of a mixture of evil and goodness in unknown proportions, no one can tell what effects he should expect from his own actions.

5
A Prophetic History of the Human Race Must Nevertheless Start from Some Sort of Experience

In human affairs, there must be some experience or other which, as an event which has actually occurred, might suggest that man has the quality or power of being the *cause* and (since his actions are supposed to be those of a being endowed with freedom) the *author* of his own improvement. But an event can be predicted as the effect of a given cause only when the circumstances which help to shape it actually arise. And while it can well be predicted in general that these circumstances must arise at some time or another (as in calculating probabilities in games of chance), it is impossible to determine whether this will happen during my lifetime, and whether I shall myself experience it and thus be able to confirm the original prediction.

We must therefore search for an event which would indicate that such a cause exists and that it is causally active within the human race, irrespective of the time at which it might actually operate; and it would have to be a cause which allowed us to conclude, as an inevitable consequence of its operation, that mankind is improving. This inference could then be extended to cover the history of former times so as to show that mankind has always been progressing, yet in such a way that the event originally chosen as an example would not in itself be regarded as the cause of progress in the past, but only as a rough indication or *historical sign* (*signum rememorativum, demonstrativum, prognostikon*). It might then serve to prove the existence of a *tendency* within the human race as a *whole*, considered not as a series of individuals (for this would result in interminable enumerations and calculations) but as a body distributed over the earth in states and national groups.

6

An Occurrence in our Own Times Which Proves This Moral Tendency of the Human Race

The occurrence in question does not involve any of those momentous deeds or misdeeds of men which make small in their eyes what was formerly great or make great what was formerly small, and which cause ancient and illustrious states to vanish as if by magic, and others to arise in their place as if from the bowels of the earth. No, it has nothing to do with all this. We are here concerned only with the attitude of the onlookers as it reveals itself *in public* while the drama of great political changes is taking place: for they openly express universal yet disinterested sympathy for one set of protagonists against their adversaries, even at the risk that their partiality could be of great disadvantage to themselves. Their reaction (because of its universality) proves that mankind as a whole shares a certain character in common, and it also proves (because of its disinterestedness) that man has a moral character, or at least the makings of one. And this does not merely allow us to hope for human improvement; it is already a form of improvement in itself, in so far as its influence is strong enough for the present.

The revolution which we have seen taking place in our own times in a nation of gifted people may succeed, or it may fail. It may be so filled with misery and atrocities that no right-thinking man would ever decide to make the same experiment again at such a price, even if he could hope to carry it out successfully at the second attempt. But I maintain that this revolution has aroused in the hearts and desires of all spectators who are not themselves caught up in it a *sympathy* which borders almost on enthusiasm, although the very utterance of this sympathy was fraught with danger. It cannot therefore have been caused by anything other than a moral disposition within the human race.

The moral cause which is at work here is composed of two elements. Firstly, there is the *right* of every people to give itself a civil constitution of the kind that it sees fit, without interference from other powers. And secondly, once it is accepted that the only intrinsically *rightful* and morally good constitution which a people can have is by its very nature disposed to avoid wars of aggression (i.e. that the only possible constitution is a republican one, at least in its conception),[19] there is the *aim*, which is also a duty, of submitting to those conditions by which war, the source of all evils and moral corruption, can be prevented. If this aim is recognized, the human race, for all its frailty, has a negative guarantee that it will progressively improve or at least that it will not be disturbed in its progress.

All this, along with the *passion* or *enthusiasm* with which men embrace the cause of goodness (although the former cannot be entirely applauded, since all passion as such is blameworthy), gives historical support for the following assertion, which is of considerable anthropological significance: true enthusiasm is always directed exclusively towards the *ideal*, particularly towards that which is purely moral (such as the concept of right), and it cannot be coupled with selfish interests. No pecuniary rewards could inspire the opponents of the revolutionaries with that zeal and greatness of soul which the concept of right could alone produce in them, and even the old military aristocracy's concept of honour (which is analogous to enthusiasm) vanished before the arms of those who had fixed their gaze on the *rights* of the people to which they belonged,[20] and who regarded themselves as its protectors. And then the external public of onlookers sympathized with their exaltation, without the slightest intention of actively participating in their affairs.

7

The Prophetic History of Mankind

In these principles, there must be something *moral* which reason recognizes not only as pure, but also (because of its great and epoch-making influence) as something to

77

which the human soul manifestly acknowledges a duty. Moreover, it concerns the human race as a complete association of men (*non singulorum, sed universorum* ['Not of individuals, but of mankind as a whole']), for they rejoice with universal and disinterested sympathy at its anticipated success and at all attempts to make it succeed.

The occurrence in question is not, however, a phenomenon of revolution, but (as Erhard puts it) of the *evolution* of a constitution governed by *natural right*. Such a constitution cannot itself be achieved by furious struggles – for civil and foreign wars will destroy whatever *statutory* order has hitherto prevailed – but it does lead us to strive for a constitution which would be incapable of bellicosity, i.e. a republican one. The actual *form* of the desired state might be republican, or alternatively, it might only be republican in its *mode of government*, in that the state would be administered by a single ruler (the monarch) acting by analogy with the laws which a people would give itself in conformity with universal principles of right.

Even without the mind of a seer, I now maintain that I can predict from the aspects and signs of our times that the human race will achieve this end, and that it will henceforth progressively improve without any more total reversals. For a phenomenon of this kind which has taken place in human history *can never be forgotten*, since it has revealed in human nature an aptitude and power for improvement of a kind which no politician could have thought up by examining the course of events in the past. Only nature and freedom, combined within mankind in accordance with principles of right, have enabled us to forecast it; but the precise time at which it will occur must remain indefinite and dependent upon chance.

But even if the intended object behind the occurrence we have described were not to be achieved for the present, or if a people's revolution or constitutional reform were ultimately to fail, or if, after the latter had lasted for a certain time, everything were to be brought back onto its original course (as politicians now claim to prophesy), our own philosophical prediction still loses none of its force. For the occurrence in question is too momentous, too intimately interwoven with the interests of humanity and too widespread in its influence upon all parts of the world for nations not to be reminded of it when favourable circumstances present themselves, and to rise up and make renewed attempts of the same kind as before. After all, since it is such an important concern of the human race, the intended constitution must at some time or another finally reach that degree of stability which the lessons of repeated experience will not fail to instil into the hearts of everyone.

Thus the proposition that the human race has always been progressively improving and will continue to develop in the same way is not just a well-meant saying to be recommended for practical purposes. Whatever unbelievers may say, it is tenable within the most strictly theoretical context. And if one considers not only the events which may happen within a particular nation, but also their repercussions upon all the nations of the earth which might gradually begin to participate in them, a view opens up into the unbounded future. This would not be true, of course, if the first epoch of natural convulsions, which (according to Camper and Blumenbach) engulfed the animal and vegetable kingdoms before the era of man, were to be followed by a second in which the human race were given the same treatment so that other creatures might take the stage instead, etc. For man in turn is a mere trifle in relation to the omnipotence of nature, or rather to its inaccessible highest cause. But if the rulers of man's own species regard him as such and treat him accordingly, either by burdening him like a beast and using him as a mere instrument of their ends, or by setting him up to fight in their disputes and slaughter his fellows, it is not just a trifle but a reversal of the *ultimate purpose* of creation.

8

The Difficulty of Maxims Directed Towards the World's Progressive Improvement as Regards Their Publicity

Popular enlightenment is the public instruction of the people upon their duties and rights towards the state to which they belong. Since this concerns only natural rights and rights which can be derived from ordinary common sense, their obvious exponents and interpreters among the people will not be officials appointed by the state, but free teachers of right, i.e. the philosophers. The latter, on account of the very freedom which they allow themselves, are a stumbling-block to the state, whose only wish is to rule; they are accordingly given the appellation of 'enlighteners', and decried as a menace to the state. And yet they do not address themselves in familiar tones to the *people* (who themselves take little or no notice of them and their writings), but in *respectful* tones to the state, which is thereby implored to take the rightful needs of the people to heart. And if a whole people wishes to present its grievance (*gravamen*), the only way in which this can be done is by publicity. A ban on publicity will therefore hinder a nation's progress, even with regard to the least of its claims, the claim for natural rights.

Another thing which is concealed (transparently enough) by legal measures from a certain people is the true nature of its constitution. It would be an affront to the majesty of the people of Great Britain to say that they lived under an *absolute monarchy*. Instead, it is said that their constitution is one which *limits* the will of the monarch through the two houses of parliament, acting as representatives of the people. Yet everyone knows very well that the influence of the monarch upon these represenatives is so great and so infallible that the aforesaid houses make no decisions except those which His Majesty wishes and recommends through his minister. Now and again, the latter will certainly recommend decisions wherein he knows and indeed *ensures* that he will meet with contradiction (as with the abolition of the slave trade), simply in order to furnish ostensible proof of parliamentary freedom. But this sort of approach has the insidious effect of discouraging people from looking for the true and rightfully established constitution, for they imagine they have discovered it in an instance which is already before them. Thus a mendacious form of publicity deceives the people with the illusion that the monarchy is *limited*[21] by a law which emanates from them, while their representatives, won over by bribery, secretly subject them to an *absolute monarch*.

All forms of state are based on the idea of a constitution which is compatible with the natural rights of man, so that those who obey the law should also act as a unified body of legislators. And if we accordingly think of the commonwealth in terms of concepts of pure reason, it may be called a Platonic *ideal* (*respublica noumenon*), which is not an empty figment of the imagination, but the eternal norm for all civil constitutions whatsoever, and a means of ending all wars. A civil society organized in conformity with it and governed by laws of freedom is an example representing it in the world of experience (*respublica phaenomenon*), and it can only be achieved by a laborious process, after innumerable wars and conflicts. But its constitution, once it has been attained as a whole, is the best qualified of all to keep out war, the destroyer of everything good. Thus it is our duty to enter into a constitution of this kind; and in the meantime, since it will be a considerable time before this takes place, it is the duty of monarchs to govern in a *republican* (not a democratic) manner, even although they may *rule autocratically*. In other words, they should treat the people in accordance with principles akin in spirit to the laws of freedom which a people of mature rational powers would prescribe for itself, even if the people is not literally asked for its consent.

9

What Profit will the Human Race Derive from Progressive Improvement?

The profit which will accrue to the human race as it works its way forward will not be an ever increasing quantity of *morality* in its attitudes. Instead, the *legality* of its attitudes will produce an increasing number of actions governed by duty, whatever the particular motive behind these actions may be. In other words, the profit will result from man's good *deeds* as they grow ever more numerous and successful, i.e. from the external phenomena of man's moral nature. For we have only *empirical* data (our experiences) on which to base this prediction – that is, we base it on the physical cause of our actions in so far as they actually take place as phenomena, not on the moral cause which contains the concept of duty as applied to what ought to happen, and which can be determined by processes of pure *a priori* thinking.

Violence will gradually become less on the part of those in power, and obedience towards the laws will increase. There will no doubt be more charity, less quarrels in legal actions, more reliability in keeping one's word, and so on in the commonwealth, partly from a love of honour, and partly from a lively awareness of where one's own advantage lies; and this will ultimately extend to the external relations between the various peoples, until a cosmopolitan society is created. Such developments do not mean, however, that the basic moral capacity of mankind will increase in the slightest, for this would require a kind of new creation or supernatural influence. For we must not expect too much of human beings in their progressive improvements, or else we shall merit the scorn of those politicians who would gladly treat man's hopes of progress as the fantasies of an overheated mind.[22]

10
What Sequence can Progress be Expected to Follow?

The answer is: not the usual sequence *from the bottom upwards*, but *from the top downwards*.

To expect that the education of young people in intellectual and moral culture, reinforced by the doctrines of religion, firstly through domestic instruction and then through a series of schools from the lowest to the highest grade, will eventually not only make them good citizens, but will also bring them up to practise a kind of goodness which can continually progress and maintain itself, is a plan which is scarcely likely to achieve the desired success. For on the one hand, the people believe that the expense of educating their children should be met not by them but by the state; and on the other, the state itself (as Büsching laments) has no money left over to pay qualified teachers who will carry out their duties with enthusiasm, since it needs it all for war. But apart from this, the whole mechanism of education as described above will be completely disjointed unless it is designed on the considered plan and intention of the highest authority in the state, then set in motion and constantly maintained in uniform operation thereafter. And this will mean that the state too will reform itself from time to time, pursuing evolution instead of revolution, and will thus make continuous progress. But those responsible for the desired education are also *human beings* who will therefore have to have had a suitable education themselves. And in view of the frailty of human nature and the fortuitous circumstances which can intensify its effects, we can expect man's hopes of progress to be fulfilled only under the positive condition of a higher wisdom (which, if it is invisible to us, is known as providence); and in so far as *human beings* can themselves accomplish anything or anything can be expected of them, it can only be through their negative wisdom in furthering their own ends. In the latter event, they will find themselves compelled to ensure that *war*, the greatest obstacle to morality and the invariable enemy of progress, first becomes gradually more humane, then more infrequent, and finally disappears completely as a mode of aggression. They will thereby enter into a constitution based on genuine principles of right, which is by its very nature capable of constant progress and improvement without forfeiting its strength.

Conclusion

A doctor who used to console his patients from day to day with hopes of imminent recovery, telling one that his pulse was better, and others that their faeces or perspiration heralded an improvement, etc., received a visit from one of his friends. 'How are you, my friend, and how is your illness?' was the first question. 'How do you think,' was the reply. *'I am dying of sheer recovery!'*

I do not blame anyone if political evils make him begin to despair of the welfare and progress of mankind. But I have confidence in the heroic medicine to which Hume refers, for it ought to produce a speedy cure. 'When I now see the nations engaged in war', he says, 'it is as if I witnessed two drunken wretches bludgeoning each other in a china-shop. For it is not just that the injuries they inflict on each other will be long in healing; they will also have to pay for all the damage they have caused.' *Sero sapiunt Phryges* ['The Phrygians learn wisdom too late']. But the after-pains of the present war will force the political prophet to admit that the human race must soon take a turn for the better, and this turn is now already in sight.

Conjectures on the Beginning of Human History

To *introduce* conjectures at various points in the *course* of a historical account in order to fill gaps in the record is surely permissible; for what comes before and after these gaps – i.e. the remote cause and the effect respectively – can enable us to discover the intermediate causes with reasonable certainty, thereby rendering the intervening process intelligible. But to *base* a historical account solely on conjectures would seem little better than drawing up a plan for a novel. Indeed, such an account could not be described as a *conjectural history* at all, but merely as a *work of fiction.* – Nevertheless, what it may be presumptuous to introduce in the course of a history of human actions may well be permissible with reference to the *first beginning* of that history, for if the beginning is a product of *nature*, it may be discoverable by conjectural means. In other words, it does not have to be invented but can be deduced from experience, assuming that what was experienced at the beginning of history was no better or worse than what is experienced now – an assumption which accords with the analogy of nature and which has nothing presumptuous about it. Thus, a history of the first development of freedom from its origins as a predisposition in human nature is something quite different from a history of its subsequent course, which must be based exclusively on historical records.

Nevertheless, conjectures should not make undue claims on our assent. On the contrary, they should not present themselves as a serious activity but merely as an exercise in which the imagination, supported by reason, may be allowed to indulge as a healthy mental recreation. Consequently, they cannot stand comparison with a historical account which is put forward and accepted as a genuine record of the same event, a record which is tested by criteria quite different from those derived merely from the philosophy of nature. For this very reason, and because the journey on which I am about to venture is no more than a pleasure trip, I may perhaps hope to be granted permission to employ a sacred document as my map, and at the same time to speculate that the journey which I shall make on the wings of imagination – although not without the guidance of experience as mediated by reason – will follow precisely the same course as that which the sacred text records as history. The reader will have the document in question before him (Genesis, Chapters II–VI), and may consult it at every step to see whether the route which philosophy follows with the help of concepts accords with that which the Bible story describes.

If we are not to indulge in wild conjectures, we must begin with something which human reason cannot deduce from prior natural causes – that is, with the *existence of human beings*. These human beings must also be *fully developed*, for they have no mother to support them, and they must be a *pair* in order that they may reproduce their kind. Besides, there must be only *one* couple if war is not to break out at once – as would happen if the people in question were close to one another yet strangers – and if nature is not to be accused of having failed, by permitting descent from different ancestors, to take the most appropriate measures to promote sociability as the principal end of human destiny; for the common descent of all human beings from a single family unit was undoubtedly the best means of attaining this end. I then place this couple in a setting secure from the attacks of wild beasts and amply provided by nature with every means of sustenance – a *garden*, so to speak, in a climate of constant mildness. What is more, I imagine them not in their wholly primitive natural state, but only after they have made significant advances in the skilful use of their powers. For the reader might well find too many conjectures and too few probabilities if I were to try to fill this gap, which presumably occupied a considerable interval of time. The first human being could therefore *stand* and *walk*; he could *speak* (cf. Genesis 11. 20)[23] and indeed *talk* – i.e. speak with the help of coherent concepts (11. 23) – and consequently *think*. These are all skills which he had to acquire for himself (for if they were innate, they would also be inherited, which does not tally with experience); I assume, however, that he is already in possession of them, for I wish merely to consider the development of human behaviour from the ethical point of view, and this necessarily presupposes that the skills in question are already present.

Initially, the newcomer must have been guided solely by instinct, that *voice of God* which all animals obey. It permitted him to use some things as food and forbade him to use others (III. 2–3). – It is unnecessary, however, to assume for this purpose a particular instinct which has now been lost. It could simply have been the sense of smell and its affinity with the organ of taste, along with that sympathy which is known to exist between the latter and the digestive organs – in other words an ability, which is still in evidence today, to sense in advance whether a given food is suitable for consumption or not. We need not even assume that this sense was more acute in the first couple than it is now; for it is common knowledge that the perceptive powers of those who employ only their senses differ greatly from those of people who are also engaged in thought, and who accordingly pay less attention to their sensations.

So long as inexperienced man obeyed this call of nature, his lot was a happy one. But *reason* soon made its presence felt and sought to extend his knowledge of foodstuffs beyond the bounds of instinct; it did so by comparing his usual diet with anything which a sense other than that to which his instinct was tied – for example, the sense of sight – represented as similar in character (III. 6). Even if instinct did not recommend it, this experiment had a chance of succeeding so long as instinct did not contradict it. But it is a peculiarity of reason that it is able, with the help of the imagination, to invent desires which not only *lack* any corresponding natural impulse, but which are even *at variance* with the latter. Such desires, which are known primarily as *lasciviousness*, gradually engender a whole host of superfluous or even unnatural inclinations to which the term *luxuriousness* applies. The initial incentive to abandon natural impulses may have been quite trivial. But the outcome of that first experiment whereby man became conscious of his reason as a faculty which can extend beyond the limits to which all animals are confined was of great importance, and it influenced his way of life decisively. Thus, it may have been only a fruit which, because it looked similar to other agreeable fruits which he had previously tasted, encouraged him to make the experiment. There may also have been the example of an animal to which such food was naturally congenial, although it had an opposite and harmful effect on human beings, whose natural instinct was consequently opposed to it. Nevertheless, this was enough to give reason the initial inducement to quibble with the voice of nature (III. 1), and despite the latter's objections, to make the first experiment in free choice – an experiment which, since it was the first, probably did not turn out as expected. No matter how trivial the harm it did may have been, it was nevertheless enough to open man's eyes (III. 7). He discovered in himself an ability to choose his own way of life without being tied to any single one like the other animals. But the momentary gratification which this realization of his superiority may have afforded him was inevitably followed at once by anxiety and fear as to how he should employ his newly discovered ability, given that he did not yet know the hidden properties or remote effects of anything. He stood, as it were, on the edge of an abyss. For whereas instinct had hitherto directed him towards individual objects of his desire, an infinite range of objects now opened up, and he did not yet know how to choose between them. Yet now that he had tasted this state of freedom, it was impossible for him to return to a state of servitude under the rule of instinct.

Next to the instinct for food by which nature preserves each individual, the *sexual instinct*, by which nature ensures the survival of each species, is the most prominent. Once reason had awakened, it was not slow to make its influence felt in this area either. Man soon discovered that the sexual stimulus, which in the case of animals is based merely on a transient and largely periodic urge, could in his case be prolonged and even increased by means of the imagination. For although the imagination performs its function with greater moderation the further its object is *withdrawn from the senses*, it also functions more constantly and uniformly, thereby avoiding that satiety which follows the satisfaction of a purely animal desire. The fig-leaf was accordingly the product of a much stronger assertion of reason than had been evident in the first phase of its development. For to render an inclination more intense and lasting by withdrawing its object from the senses already displays a consciousness of some rational control over the impulses, and not just an ability, as in the first stage of rationality, to obey the impulses to a greater or lesser extent. *Refusal* was the device which invested purely sensuous stimuli with an ideal quality, and which gradually showed the way from purely animal desire to love, and so also from a feeling for the merely agreeable to a taste for beauty (initially only in human form, but subsequently also in nature). Furthermore, the first incentive for man's development as a moral being came from his *sense of decency*, his inclination to inspire respect in others by good manners (i.e. by concealing all that might invite contempt) as the proper foundation of all true sociability. – A small beginning such as this, which nevertheless has epoch-making effects in imparting a wholly new direction to thought, is more important than the whole endless series of subsequent cultural developments.

The third step which reason took after its intervention in man's basic and immediately felt needs was to reflect in *anticipation of the future*. This ability not just to enjoy the present moment of life but also to visualize what is yet to come, often in the distant future, is the most decisive proof of man's advantage, in that he is able to prepare for remote objectives in keeping with his destiny. But this same ability is also the most inexhaustible source of cares and worries which an uncertain future evokes, and from which all animals are exempt (III. 13–19). The man who had to provide for himself, his wife, and his future children foresaw the increasing laboriousness of his work; the woman foresaw the hardships to which nature had subjected her sex, as well as those which the more powerful man would inflict upon her. Both foresaw with apprehension, at the end of a life of toil and as yet in the background of the picture, the fate which must befall all animals but which causes them no concern, namely death; and they seemed to reproach themselves for, and regard as a crime, that use of reason which had brought all these ills upon them. Perhaps the only comfort and reassurance they had was the prospect of living through their offspring, whose lot might be better than theirs or who might even, as members of one family, alleviate their parents' troubles (III. 16–20).

The fourth and last step which reason took, thereby raising man completely above animal society, was his (albeit obscure) realization that he is the true *end of nature*, and that nothing which lives on earth can compete with him in this respect. When he first said to the sheep *'the fleece which you wear was given to you by nature not for your own use, but for mine'* and took it from the sheep to wear it himself (III. 21), he became aware of a prerogative which, by his nature, he enjoyed over all the animals; and he now no longer regarded them as fellow creatures, but as means and instruments to be used at will for the attainment of whatever ends he pleased. This notion implies (if only obscurely) an awareness of the following distinction: man should not address other *human beings* in the same way as animals, but should regard them as having an equal share in the gifts of nature. This was a distant preparation for those restrictions which reason would in future impose on man's will in relation to his fellows, a preparation which is much more essential for the establishment of society than is inclination or love.

Thus, man had attained a position of *equality with all rational beings*, whatever their rank (III. 22), because he could claim *to be an end in himself*, to be accepted as such by all others, and not to be used by anyone else simply as a means to other ends. This, rather than reason considered merely as an instrument for the satisfaction of various inclinations, is the basis of man's unconditional equality even with higher beings; for even if the latter are incomparably superior to him in natural gifts, they do not have a right to use him as they please. Consequently, this fourth step of reason is also associated with man's *release* from the womb of nature, a change of status which undoubtedly does him honour, but is at the same time fraught with danger; for it expelled him from the harmless and secure condition of a protected childhood – from a garden, as it were, which provided for him without any effort on his part (III. 23) – and thrust him out into the world at large, where so many cares, labours, and unknown evils awaited him. In the future, the hardships of life would often arouse in him the wish for a paradise created by his imagination, a paradise where he could dream or idle away his existence in quiet inactivity and everlasting peace. But restless reason, irresistibly driving him on to develop his innate capacities, stands between him and that imagined seat of bliss, and does not allow him to return to the state of rude simplicity from which it had originally extracted him (III. 24). It urges him to submit patiently to the labours he detests, to pursue the trivialities he despises, and to forget even his terror of death in favour of all those trifles whose loss he fears even more.

Note

From this account of the earliest history of man, the following conclusion can be drawn. Man's emergence from that paradise which reason represents to him as the first abode of his species was nothing other than his transition from a rude and purely animal existence to a state of humanity, from the leading-strings of instinct to the guidance of reason – in a word, from the guardianship of nature to the state of freedom. Whether he gained or lost through this change is no longer a question when we consider the destiny of his species, which consists quite simply in *progress* towards perfection, however flawed his first attempts to attain this end – even if they are followed by a long series of further attempts – may prove to be. – But while this course represents a *progression* from worse to better for the species as a whole, this is not so in the case of the individual. Before reason awoke, there were no commandments or prohibitions, so that violations of these were also impossible. But when reason began to function and, in all its weakness, came into conflict with animality in all its strength, evils necessarily ensued; and even worse, as reason grew more cultivated, vices emerged which were quite foreign to the state of ignorance and hence of innocence. From the moral point of view, therefore, the first step beyond this state was a *fall*; and from the physical point of view, this fall was a punishment, for it led to a host of hitherto unknown evils. Thus, the history of *nature* begins with goodness, for it is the *work of God*; but the history of *freedom* begins with evil, for it is the *work of man*. For the individual, who looks only to himself in the exercise of his freedom, a change of this kind represented a loss; for nature, whose end in relation to man concerns the species, it represented a gain. The individual therefore has cause to blame himself for all the ills which he endures and for all the evil which he perpetrates; but at the same time, as the member of a whole (of a species), he has cause to admire and praise the wisdom and purposiveness of the overall arrangement. – In this way, it is possible to reconcile with each other and with reason the often misunderstood and apparently contradictory pronouncements of the celebrated *J. J. Rousseau*. In his esays *On the Influence of the Sciences* and *On the Inequality of Man*, he shows quite correctly that there is an inevitable conflict between culture and the nature of the human race as a *physical* species each of whose individual members is meant to fulfil his destiny completely. But in his *Émile*, his *Social Contract*, and other writings, he attempts in turn to solve the more difficult problem of what course culture should take in order to ensure the proper development, in keeping with their destiny, of man's capacities as a *moral* species, so that this [moral] destiny will no longer conflict with his character as a natural species. Since culture has perhaps not yet really begun – let alone completed – its development in accordance with the true principles of man's *education* as a human being and citizen, the above conflict is the source of all the genuine evils which oppress human life, and of all the vices which dishonour it.[24] At the same time, the very impulses which are blamed as the causes of vice are good in themselves, fulfilling their function as abilities implanted by nature. But since these abilities are adapted to the state of nature, they are undermined by the advance of culture and themselves undermine the latter in turn, until art, when it reaches perfection, once more becomes nature – and this is the ultimate goal of man's moral destiny.

The End of History

The following period began with man's transition from the age of leisure and peace to the age of *labour and discord* as the prelude to social union. Here, we must make another major leap and suddenly put him in possession of domestic animals and of crops which he can propagate himself for his own consumption by sowing and planting (IV. 2). In fact, the transition from the savage life of the hunter to the former [pastoral] state, and from sporadic digging for roots or gathering of fruit to the second [agricultural] state, may have taken place very gradually. It was at this point that strife inevitably arose between those who had hitherto lived together in peace, with the result that those whose ways of life were different became separated and dispersed throughout the world. *Pastoral life* is not only leisurely, but also the most reliable means of support, for there is no lack of fodder for animals in a largely uninhabited country. *Agriculture* or the planting of crops, on the other hand, is extremely laborious, subject to the vagaries of climate, and consequently insecure; it also requires permanent settlements, ownership of land, and sufficient strength to defend the latter. The herdsman, however, abhors such property because it limits his freedom of pasture. As far as agriculture is concerned, the farmer may have seemed to envy the herdsman as someone more favoured by heaven

(IV. 4); but in fact, the herdsman caused him great inconvenience so long as he remained in the neighbourhood,
for grazing animals do not spare the farmer's crops. It is
also easy for the herdsman to move further afield with
his animals, thus avoiding the need to make any resti-
tution for the damage he has done, for he leaves nothing
behind which he could not just as easily find elsewhere.
Thus, the farmer no doubt had to use force to prevent
these incursions, which were not considered unlawful
by his adversary; and since the cause of such incursions
could never be entirely eliminated, he was no doubt
eventually compelled to *distance* himself as far as possible
from those who lived a pastoral existence, unless he
wished to lose the fruits of his long and diligent efforts
(IV. 16). This separation marks the beginning of the third
epoch.

Where people depend for their livelihood on the cultivation of the soil (and on the planting of trees in particular), they require permanent accommodation; and the
defence of such property against all encroachment requires a large number of people who are prepared to
assist one another. Hence those who adopted this way
of life could no longer live in scattered family units, but
had to stick together and set up village communities
(incorrectly described as *towns*) in order to protect their
property against savage hunters or tribes of pastoral
nomads. The first essentials of life which a *changed mode
of living* makes necessary (IV. 20) could now be acquired
by mutual *exchange*. This inevitably gave rise to *culture*
and the beginnings of *art*, both as a pastime and as an
occupation (IV. 21f); but first and foremost, it also meant

that certain steps were taken to establish a civil constitution and the public administration of justice. Initially,
the latter was no doubt concerned only with major acts
of violence, the avenging of which was now no longer
left to individuals as in the savage state, but assigned to
a lawful authority which served to unite the whole –
i.e. to a kind of government which was not itself subject
to the rule of force (IV. 23f.). – From these first crude
beginnings, all human aptitudes could now gradually
develop, the most beneficial of these being *sociability and
civil security*. The human race could multiply and, like a
beehive, send out colonists in all directions from the
centre – colonists who were already civilized. This epoch
also saw the beginning of human *inequality*, that abund-
ant source of so much evil but also of everything good;
this inequality continued to increase thereafter.

So long as the nations of nomadic herdsmen, who
recognize only God as their master, continued to swarm
around the town-dwellers and farmers, who are governed by a human master or civil authority (VI. 4),[25] and,
as declared enemies of all land ownership, treated the
latter with hostility and were hated by them in turn, the
two sides were continually at war, or at least at constant
risk of war. But as a consequence, both nations could at
least enjoy the priceless asset of internal freedom. (For
even now, the risk of war is the only thing which keeps
despotism in check, because a state must now have
wealth before it can be powerful, and there can be no
wealth-producing activity without *freedom*. In a poor
nation, this lack of wealth must be compensated for by
widespread efforts to preserve the commonwealth, and

this is again impossible unless the nation feels that such efforts can be freely made.) – In the course of time, however, the growing luxury of the town-dwellers, and in particular the seductive arts in which the women of the towns surpassed the unkempt wenches of the wilderness, must have been a powerful temptation to the herdsmen to enter into relations with them and to let themselves be drawn into the glittering misery of the towns (VI. 2). The consequent amalgamation of two formerly hostile populations put an end to the danger of war, but it also put an end to freedom. This led on the one hand to a despotism of powerful tyrants, and – since culture had only just begun – to soulless extravagance and the most abject slavery, combined with all the vices of the uncivilized state. On the other hand, the human race was irresistibly deflected from the course marked out for it by nature, namely the progressive cultivation of its capacities for goodness. It thus became unworthy of its very existence as a species whose destiny was to rule over the earth rather than to live in brutish indulgence and grovelling servitude (VI. 17).

Concluding Note

Thinking people are subject to a malaise which may even turn into moral corruption, a malaise of which the unthinking are ignorant – namely discontent with that providence by which the course of the world as a whole is governed. They feel this sentiment when they contemplate the evils which so greatly oppress the human race, with no hope (as it seems) of any improvement. Yet it is of the utmost importance *that we should be content with providence*, even if the path it has laid out for us on earth is an arduous one. We should be content with it partly in order that we may take courage even in the midst of hardships, and partly in order that we should not blame all such evils on fate and fail to notice that we may ourselves be entirely responsible for them, thereby losing the chance to remedy them by improving ourselves.

We have to admit that the greatest evils which oppress civilized nations are the result of *war* – not so much of actual wars in the past or present as of the unremitting, indeed ever-increasing *preparation* for war in the future. All the resources of the state, and all the fruits of its culture which might be used to enhance that culture even further, are devoted to this purpose. Freedom suffers greatly in numerous areas, and the state's maternal care for its individual members is replaced by demands of implacable harshness (even if this harshness is justified by fear of external threats). But if the constant fear of war did not compel even heads of state to show this *respect for humanity*, would we still encounter the same culture, or that close association of social classes within the commonwealth which promotes the well-being of all? Would we still encounter the same popu-lation, or even that degree of freedom which is still present in spite of highly restrictive laws? We need only look at *China*, whose position may expose it to occasional unforeseen incursions but not to attack by a powerful enemy, and we shall find that, for this very reason, it has been stripped of every vestige of freedom. – So long as human culture remains at its present stage, war is therefore an indispensable means of advancing it further; and only when culture has reached its full development – and only God knows when that will be – will perpetual peace become possible and of benefit to us. In this connection, therefore, we surely have only ourselves to blame for the evils which we so bitterly lament; and the Holy Scripture is quite justified in regarding the amalgamation of nations into one society, and their complete liberation from external danger at a time when their culture had scarcely emerged, as an obstacle to all further cultural progress and a descent into irremediable corruption.

The *second source of man's dissatisfaction* with the order of nature is the *shortness of life*. It is true that anyone who continues to wish that life might last longer than it actually does must have little appreciation of its value, for to prolong it would merely add to the length of a drama made up of endless struggles with adversity. Nevertheless, we may excuse those of childish judgement who fear death but have no love of life, and who find it hard to complete each day of their existence with some degree of contentment, yet can never have days enough in which to repeat this painful experience. But if we stop to think of all the care that afflicts us in our search for ways of passing a life as short as this, and of all the injustice that is done in the hope of a future enjoyment which will last for so short a time, it is reasonable to conclude that a life-expectancy of 800 years or more would not be to our advantage. Fathers would live in mortal fear of their sons, brothers of brothers, and friends of friends, and the vices of a human race of such longevity would necessarily reach such a pitch that it would deserve no better a fate than to be wiped from the face of the earth by a universal flood (VI. 12f.).

The *third* wish (which is in fact an empty yearning, for it knows that its object can never be attained) is a reflection of that *golden age* which poets have praised so highly. In it, we are supposedly relieved of all those imaginary needs with which luxury encumbers us, we are content with the bare necessities of nature, and there is complete equality and perpetual peace among men – in a word, there is pure enjoyment of a carefree life, frittered away in idle dreams or childish play. It is yearnings such as these which make tales of Robinson Crusoe and voyages to the South Sea islands so attractive; but in a wider sense, they are symptoms of that weariness of civilized life which thinking people feel when they seek its value in *pleasure* alone, and when they resort to idleness as an antidote as soon as reason reminds them that they ought to give value to their life through their *actions*. The vacuity of this wish for a return to the past age of simplicity and innocence is adequately demonstrated by the foregoing account of man's original state. For as we have seen, man cannot remain in this state because it does not satisfy him, and he is even less inclined to go back to it once he has left it. Consequently, he must continue to ascribe his present condition and all its hardships to himself and his own choice.

An account of human history will be of benefit to man and will serve to instruct and improve him if it contains the following lessons. It must show him that he should not blame providence for the evils which oppress him, and that he is not entitled to ascribe his own misdemeanours to an original crime committed by his earliest ancestors, by alleging, for example, that a disposition to commit similar offences has been passed down to their descendants; for there can be nothing inherited about arbitrary actions. It should show him instead that he has every justification for acknowledging the action of his first ancestors as his own, and that he should hold himself wholly responsible for all the evils which spring from the misuse of his reason; for he is quite capable of realizing that, in the same circumstances, he would have behaved in exactly the same way, in that his first act in using reason would have been to misuse it (even if nature advised him otherwise). Once this point concerning moral evils has been correctly understood, the strictly physical evils will scarcely tip the balance in our favour when merits and faults are weighed against each other.

The conclusion to be drawn from this attempt to describe the earliest history of mankind with the help of philosophy is therefore as follows. We should be content with providence and with the course of human affairs as a whole, which does not begin with good and then proceed to evil, but develops gradually from the worse to the better; and each individual is for his own part called upon by nature itself to contribute towards this progress to the best of his ability.

Notes

1. I read today on the 30th September in Büsching's *Wöchentliche Nachrichten* of 13th September a notice concerning this month's *Berlinische Monatsschrift*. The notice mentions Mendelssohn's answer to the same question as that which I have answered. I have not yet seen this journal, otherwise I should have held back the above reflections. I let them stand only as a means of finding out by comparison how far the thoughts of two individuals may coincide by chance.

2. A hereditary kingdom is not a state which can be inherited by another state. Only the right to rule over it may be bequeathed to another physical person. In this case, the state acquires a ruler, but the ruler as such (i.e. as one who already has another kingdom) does not acquire the state.

3. It has hitherto been doubted, not without justification, whether there can be permissive laws (*leges permissivae*) in addition to preceptive laws (*leges praeceptivae*) and prohibitive laws (*leges prohibitivae*). For all laws embody an element of objective practical necessity as a reason for certain actions, whereas a permission depends only upon practical contingencies. Thus a *permissive law* would be a compulsion to do something which one cannot be compelled to do, and if the object of the law were the same as that of the permission, a contradiction would result. But in the permissive law contained in the second article above, the initial prohibition applies only to the mode of acquiring a right in the future (e.g. by inheritance), whereas the exemption from this prohibition (i.e. the permissive part of the law) applies to the state of political possessions in the present. For in accordance with a permissive law of natural right, this present state can be allowed to remain even although the state of nature has been abandoned for that of civil society. And even if these present

possessions are unlawful, they are nevertheless *honest* (*possessio puta-tiva*). A putative possession is prohibited, however, as soon as it has been recognized as such, both in the state of nature and after the subsequent transition to civil society (if the mode of acquisition is the same). And continued possession could not be permitted if the supposed acquisition had been made in the state of civil society, for it would then have to end immediately, as an offence against right, as soon as its unlawfulness had been discovered.

My intention here was merely to point out briefly to exponents of natural right the concept of a permissive law, which automatically presents itself within the systematic divisions of reason. It is especially noteworthy since it is frequently used in civil or statutory law, with the one difference that the prohibitive part of the law exists independently, and the permissive part is not included within the law itself as a limiting condition (as it ought to be), but added to cover exceptional cases. Such laws usually state that this or that is pro-hibited, *except* in cases 1, 2 or 3, and so on *ad infinitum*, for permissive clauses are only added to the law fortuitously, by a random review of particular cases, and not in accordance with any definite principle. Otherwise, the limiting conditions would have had to be included *in the actual formula of the prohibitive law*, whereby it would have become a permissive law in itself. It is therefore to be regretted that the ingenious but unsolved competition question submitted by that wise and clear-sighted gentleman, Count Windischgrätz, was so soon abandoned, for it might have solved the legal difficulty we are at present discussing. For the possibility of finding a universal formula like those of mathematics is the only true test of consistent legislation, and without it, the so-called *ius certum* must remain no more than a pious hope. Otherwise, we shall only have *general* laws (i.e. laws *valid in general*), but no universal laws (i.e. laws which are *generally valid*) such as the concept of a law seems to demand.

4. It is usually assumed that one cannot take hostile action against anyone unless one has already been actively *injured* by them. This is perfectly correct if both parties are living in a *legal civil state*. For the fact that the one has entered such a state gives the required guarantee to the other, since both are subject to the same authority. But man

(or an individual people) in a mere state of nature robs me of any such security and injures me by virtue of this very state in which he coexists with me. He may not have injured me actively (*facto*), but he does injure me by the very lawlessness of his state (*statu iniusto*), for he is a permanent threat to me, and I can require him either to enter into a common lawful state along with me or to move away from my vicinity. Thus the postulate on which all the following articles are based is that all men who can at all influence one another must adhere to some kind of civil constitution. But any legal constitution, as far as the persons who live under it are concerned, will conform to one of the three following types:

(1) a constitution based on the *civil right* of individuals within a nation (*ius civitatis*).

(2) a constitution based on the *international right* of states in their relationships with one another (*ius gentium*).

(3) a constitution based on *cosmopolitan right*, in so far as individuals and states, coexisting in an external relationship of mutual influences, may be regarded as citizens of a universal state of mankind (*ius cosmopoliticum*). This classification, with respect to the idea of a perpetual peace, is not arbitrary, but necessary. For if even one of the parties were able to influence the others physically and yet itself remained in a state of nature, there would be a risk of war, which it is precisely the aim of the above articles to prevent.

5. *Rightful (i.e. external) freedom* cannot, as is usually thought, be defined as a warrant to do whatever one wishes unless it means doing injustice to others. For what is meant by a *warrant*? It means a possibility of acting in a certain way so long as this action does not do any injustice to others. Thus the definition would run as follows: freedom is the possibility of acting in ways which do no injustice to others. That is, we do no injustice to others (no matter what we may actually do) if we do no injustice to others. Thus the definition is an empty tautology. In fact, my external and rightful *freedom* should be defined as a warrant to obey no external laws except those to which I have been able to give my own consent. Similarly, external and rightful *equality* within a state is that relationship among the citizens whereby no one can put anyone else under a legal obligation without submitting simultaneously to a law which requires that he can himself be put under the same kind of obligation by the other person. (And we do not need to define the principle of *legal* dependence, since it is always implied in the concept of a political constitution.) The validity of these innate and inalienable rights, the necessary property of mankind, is confirmed and enhanced by the principle that man may have lawful relations even with higher beings (if he believes in the latter). For he may consider himself as a citizen of a transcendental world, to which the same principles apply. And as regards my freedom, I am not under any obligation even to divine laws (which I can recognize by reason alone), except in so far as I have been able to give my own consent to them; for I can form a conception of the divine will only in terms of the law of freedom of my own reason. As for the principle of equality in relation to the most exalted being I can conceive of, apart from God (e.g. a power such as Aeon), there is no reason, if I and this higher being are both doing our duty in our own stations, why it should be my duty to obey while he should enjoy the right to command. But the reason why this principle of equality (unlike that of freedom) does not apply to a relationship towards God, is that God is the only being for whom the concept of duty ceases to be valid.

But as for the right of equality of all citizens as subjects, we may ask whether a *hereditary aristocracy* is admissible. The answer to this question will depend entirely on whether more importance is attached to the superior *rank* granted by the state to one subject over another than is attached to *merit*, or vice versa. Now it is obvious that if rank is conferred according to birth, it will be quite uncertain whether merit (skill and devotion within one's office) will accompany it; it will be tantamount to conferring a position of command upon a favoured individual without any merit on his part, and this could never be approved by the general will of the people in an original contract, which is, after all, the principle behind all rights. For it does not necessarily follow that a nobleman is also a *noble man*. And as for a nobility of office, i.e. the rank of a *higher magistracy* which can be attained by merit, the rank does not attach as a possession to the person, but to the post occupied by the person, and this does not violate the principle of equality. For when a person lays down his office, he simultaneously resigns his rank and again becomes one of the people.

6. Many have criticized the high-sounding appellations which are often bestowed on a ruler (e.g. 'the divine anointed', or 'the executor and representative of the divine will on earth') as gross and extravagant flatteries, but it seems to me without reason. Far from making the ruler of the land arrogant, they ought rather to fill his soul with humility. For if he is a man of understanding (which we must certainly assume), he will reflect that he has taken over an office which is too great for a human being, namely that of administering God's most sacred institution on earth, the rights of man; he will always live in fear of having in any way injured God's most valued possession.

7. Mallet du Pan, in his flamboyant but hollow and empty style, boasts of having at last, after many years of experience, become convinced of the truth of Pope's famous saying: 'For forms of government let fools contest; Whate'er is best administered is best.' If this means that the best administered government is the best administered, he has cracked a nut (as Swift puts it) and been rewarded with a worm. But if it means that the best administered government is also the best kind of government (i.e. the best constitution), it is completely false, for examples of good governments prove nothing whatsoever about kinds of government. Who, indeed, governed better than a Titus or a Marcus Aurelius, and yet the one left a Domitian as his successor, and the other a Commodus. And this could not have happened under a good constitution, since their unsuitability for the post of ruler was known early enough, and the power of their predecessors was great enough to have excluded them from the succession.

8. Thus a Bulgarian prince, replying to the Greek Emperor who had kindly offered to settle his dispute with him by a duel, declared: 'A smith who possesses tongs will not lift the glowing iron out of the coals with his own hands.'

9. At the end of a war, when peace is concluded, it would not be inappropriate for a people to appoint a day of atonement after the

festival of thanksgiving. Heaven would be invoked in the name of the state to forgive the human race for the great sin of which it continues to be guilty, since it will not accommodate itself to a lawful constitution in international relations. Proud of its independence, each state prefers to employ the barbarous expedient of war, although war cannot produce the desired decision on the rights of particular states. The thanksgivings for individual victories during a war, the hymns which are sung (in the style of the Israelites) to the *Lord of Hosts*, contrast no less markedly with the moral conception of a father of mankind. For besides displaying indifference to the way in which nations pursue their mutual rights (deplorable though it is), they actually rejoice at having annihilated numerous human beings or their happiness.

10. If we wish to give this great empire the name by which it calls itself (i.e. *China*, not *Sina* or any similar form), we need only consult Georgi's *Alphabetum Tibetanum*, pp. 651–654, note b in particular. According to Professor Fischer of Petersburg, it actually has no fixed name which it might apply to itself; the commonest one is still the word *Kin*, which means gold (the Tibetans, however, call this *Ser*), which explains why the emperor is called King of Gold (i.e. of the fairest land in the world). The word is apparently pronounced *Chin* in the land itself, but expressed as *Kin* by the Italian missionaries, who cannot pronounce the correct guttural sound. It can also be seen that what the Romans called the land of the people of *Ser* was in fact China, and silk was brought from there to Europe via Greater Tibet (probably crossing Lesser Tibet, Bukhara and Persia). This led to numerous speculations on the antiquity of this extraordinary state as compared with that of Hindustan, and on its relations with Tibet as well as with Japan. But the name *Sina* or *Tschina*, which neighbouring countries allegedly use of it, leads nowhere.

Perhaps the ancient but hitherto obscure community between Europe and Tibet can be explained from what Hesychius has recorded of the hierophant's cry Κονξ Ὀμπαξ (*Konx Ompax*) in the Eleusinian Mysteries (cf. *Journey of the Younger Anacharsis*, Part v, p. 447 *et seq.*). For according to Georgi's *Alphabetum Tibetanum*, the word *Concioa* means god, and it markedly resembles *Konx*, while *Pah-cio* (*ibid.*

p. 520), which the Greeks might easily have pronounced *pax*, means *promulgator legis*, the divinity which pervades the whole of nature (also called *Cencresi*, p. 177). But *Om*, which La Croze translates as *benedictus* (blessed), can scarcely mean anything other than *beatific* if applied to the deity (p. 507). When P. Francisco Orazio asked the Tibetan lamas how they conceived of god (*Concioa*), he always received the answer: '*God is the community of all the holy ones*' (i.e. the community of blessed souls, at last reunited in the deity by being reborn as lamas after numerous migrations through all kinds of bodies, and thereby transformed into beings worthy of adoration – p.223). Thus the mysterious name *Konx Ompax* might designate that holy (*Konx*), heavenly (*Om*) and wise (*Pax*) supreme being who pervades the whole world, i.e. nature personified. As used in the Greek mysteries, it may well have signified *monotheism* to the epopts, as distinct from the *polytheism* of the uninitiated mass, although it savoured of atheism to P. Orazio (*loc. cit.*). Our earlier considerations should help to explain how this mysterious name reached the Greeks from Tibet; conversely, this influence makes it appear probable that Europe at an early date had contact with China by way of Tibet, perhaps even earlier than with India.

11. In the mechanism of nature, of which man (as a sensory being) is a part, there is evident a fundamental form on which its very existence depends. This form becomes intelligible to us only if we attribute it to the design of a universal creator who has determined it in advance. We call this predetermining influence divine *providence*, and further define it as *original providence* in so far as it is active from the earliest times onwards (*providentia conditrix; semel iussit, semper parent* [As soon as he has given the command, they obey without fail] – Augustine). In as much as it sustains the course of nature in accordance with purposive universal laws, we call it *ruling providence* (*providentia gubernatrix*). If it realizes particular ends which man could not have foreseen and whose existence can only be guessed at from the results, it is termed *guiding providence* (*providentia directrix*). And finally, if individual events are regarded as divinely intended, we no longer speak of providence but of a *special dispensation* (*directio extraordinaria*). But it is foolish presumption for man to claim that he can

recognize this as such, since it implies that a miracle has taken place, even if the events are not specifically described as miraculous. For however pious and humble it may sound, it is absurd and self-conceited for anyone to conclude from a single event that the efficient cause is governed by a special principle, or that the event in question is an end in itself and not just the natural and mechanical consequence of another end which is completely unknown to us. Similarly, it is false and self-contradictory to classify providence in terms of worldly objects (*materialiter*), dividing it up into *general* and *particular*, as occurs in the doctrine that providence takes care to preserve the various species of creatures, but leaves chance to look after the individuals; for the whole point of saying that providence applies in general is that no single object should be excepted from it. This classification, however, was probably meant to indicate that the intentions of providence are carried out *in different ways* (*formaliter*). These might be *ordinary* (e.g. the annual death and revival of nature with the changes of seasons) or *extraordinary* (e.g. the transporting of wood by Ocean currents to Arctic coasts where it cannot grow, thus providing for the native inhabitants, who could not live without it). In the latter case, while we can well explain the physico-mechanical cause of the phenomena in question (e.g. by the fact that the river-banks in temperate lands are covered in forests, so that the trees may fall into the rivers and be carried further afield by currents like the Gulf Stream), we must not on the other hand overlook teleology, which indicates the foresight of a wise agency governing nature. But the conception, current in the academic world, of a divine *participation* or *collaboration* (*concursus*) in effects experienced in the world of the senses, is superfluous. For *firstly*, it is self-contradictory to try to harness disparates together (*gryphes iungere equis* [to harness griffins with horses]), and to imply that a being who is himself the complete cause of the world's developments has to *supplement* his own predetermining providence during the course of world events (so that it must originally have been inadequate); for example, it is absurd to say that after God, the doctor acted as an assistant in curing the patient – *causa solitaria non invat* [a single cause does not suffice]. God is the creator of the doctor and of all his medicaments, so that the effect must be ascribed *entirely* to him if we are to ascend to that supreme original cause which is theoretically beyond our comprehension. Alternatively, it can be ascribed *entirely* to the doctor, in so far as we treat the event in question as belonging to the order of nature and as capable of explanation within the causal series of earthly occurrences. And *secondly*, if we adopt such attitudes, we are deprived of all definite principles by which we might judge effects. But the concept of a divine *concursus* is completely acceptable and indeed necessary in the moral and practical sense, which refers exclusively to the transcendental world. For example, we may say that we should never cease to strive towards goodness, for we believe that God, even by means which we cannot comprehend, will make up for our own lack of righteousness so long as our attitude is sincere. It is, however, self-evident that no one should use such arguments to *explain* a good deed, regarded as a secular event, for this would presuppose theoretical knowledge of the transcendental, which it is absurd for us to claim.

12. Of all ways of life, that of the hunter is undoubtedly most at odds with a civilized constitution. For families, having to live in separation, soon become strangers to each other, and subsequently, being scattered about in wide forests, they treat each other with hostility, since each requires a large area to provide itself with food and clothing. The command addressed to Noah forbidding the eating of blood (Genesis 9, 4–6) seems to have been originally nothing else but a prohibition of the hunter's way of life. For this must often involve eating uncooked meat, and if the latter is forbidden, the first is automatically ruled out too. This prohibition, often reiterated, was a condition later imposed by the Jewish Christians upon the newly accepted Christians of heathen origin, albeit with a different intention (Acts 15, 20 and 21, 25).

13. The following question might be raised. If nature intended that these frozen shores should not remain uninhabited, what will happen to their inhabitants if nature, as indeed may well happen, ceases to provide them with driftwood? For we may well believe that the natives of temperate zones, as their culture progresses, will make better use of the wood which grows on the banks of their rivers, and

will not allow it to fall into them and be swept out to sea. I should reply that those who live on the Ob, the Yenisei, the Lena etc. will supply them with it commercially, bartering it for the animal products in which the Arctic coasts are so plentiful – but only after nature has compelled them to live in peace with one another.

14. *Religious differences* – an odd expression! As if we were to speak of different *moralities*. There may certainly be different historical *confessions*, although these have nothing to do with religion itself but only with changes in the means used to further religion, and are thus the province of historical research. And there may be just as many different religious *books* (the Zend-Avesta, the Vedas, the Koran, etc.). But there can only be *one religion* which is valid for all men and at all times. Thus the different confessions can scarcely be more than the vehicles of religion; these are fortuitous, and may vary with differences in time or place.

15. These are permissive laws of reason, which allow a state of public right to continue, even if it is affected by injustice, until all is ripe for a complete revolution or has been prepared for it by peaceful means. For any *legal* constitution, even if it is only in small measure *lawful*, is better than none at all, and the fate of a premature reform would be anarchy. Thus political prudence, with things as they are at present, will make it a duty to carry out reforms appropriate to the ideal of public right. But where revolutions are brought about by nature alone, it will not use them as a good excuse for even greater oppression, but will treat them as a call of nature to create a lawful constitution based on the principles of freedom, for a thorough reform of this kind is the only one which will last.

16. It might be doubted whether any inherent wickedness rooted in human nature influences *men* who live together within a single state, for one might instead (with some plausibility) adduce the deficiencies of their as yet underdeveloped culture (i.e. their barbarism) as the cause of the unlawful elements in their thinking. But in the external relationships between *states*, this wickedness is quite undisguisedly and irrefutably apparent. Within each individual state, it is concealed by the coercion embodied in the civil laws, for the citizens' inclination to do violence to one another is counteracted by a more powerful

force – that of the government. This not only gives the whole a veneer of morality (*causae non causae*), but by putting an end to outbreaks of lawless proclivities, it genuinely makes it much easier for the moral capacities of men to develop into an immediate respect for right. For each individual believes of himself that he would by all means maintain the sanctity of the concept of right and obey it faithfully, if only he could be certain that all the others would do likewise, and the government in part guarantees this for him; thus a great step is taken *towards* morality (although this is still not the same as a moral step), towards a state where the concept of duty is recognized for its own sake, irrespective of any possible gain in return. But since each individual, despite his good opinion of himself, assumes bad faith in everyone else, men thereby pass judgement on one another to the effect that they are all in point of *fact* of little worth – although it is a moot point why this should be so, since we cannot blame it on the *nature* of man as a free being. Since, however, that respect for the concept of right which man is absolutely incapable of renouncing gives the most solemn sanction to the theory that man is also capable of conforming to this concept, everyone can see that he must himself act in accordance with it, no matter how others may behave.

17. One can find examples of such maxims in Garve's treatise *Über die Verbindung der Moral mit der Politik (On Combining Morality with Politics)*, 1788. This estimable scholar admits from the very outset that he is unable to offer a satisfactory answer to this question. But to condone such procedures while admitting that one cannot fully answer the objections which can be raised against them seems to constitute a greater concession to those who are most inclined to misuse it than it is advisable for anyone to make.

18. Those, from pythonesses to gypsies, who dabble in prophecy with neither knowledge nor honesty, are known as *false prophets*.

19. This does not mean, however, that a people which has a monarchic constitution can thereby claim the right to alter it, or even nurse a secret desire to do so. For a people which occupies extended territories in Europe may feel that monarchy is the only kind of constitution which can enable it to preserve its own existence between powerful

neighbours. And if the subjects should complain, not because of their internal government but because of their government's behaviour towards the citizens of foreign states (for example, if it were to discourage republicanism abroad), this does not prove that the people are dissatisfied with their own constitution, but rather that they are profoundly attached to it; for it becomes progressively more secure from danger as more of the other nations become republics. Nevertheless, slanderous sycophants, bent on increasing their own importance, have tried to portray this innocuous political gossip as innovationism, Jacobinism and conspiracy, constituting a menace to the state. But there was never the slightest reason for such allegations, particularly in a country more than a hundred miles removed from the scene of the revolution.

20. It may be said of such enthusiasm for asserting the rights of man: *postquam ad arma Vulcania ventum est, – mortalis mucro glacies ceu futilis ictu dissiluit* [Now that he was faced by Vulcan's arms, his mortal blade was shattered by the blow like brittle ice]. – Why has no ruler ever dared to say openly that he does not recognize any *rights* of the people against himself? Or that the people owe their happiness only to the *beneficence* of a government which confers it upon them, and that any pretensions on the part of the subject that he has rights against the government are absurd or even punishable, since they imply that resistance to authority is permissible? The reason is that any such public declaration would rouse up all the subjects against the ruler, even although they had been like docile sheep, well fed, powerfully protected and led by a kind and understanding master, and had no lack of welfare to complain of. For beings endowed with freedom cannot be content merely to enjoy the comforts of existence, which may well be provided by others (in this case, by the government); it all depends on the *principle* which governs the provision of such comforts. But welfare does not have any ruling principle, either for the recipient or for the one who provides it, for each individual will define it differently. It depends, in fact, upon the will's *material* aspect, which is empirical and thus incapable of becoming a universal rule. A being endowed with freedom, aware of the advantage he possesses over non-rational animals, can and must therefore follow

the *formal* principle of his will and demand for the people to which he belongs nothing short of a government in which the people are co-legislators. In other words, the rights of men who are expected to obey must necessarily come before all considerations of their actual wellbeing, for they are a sacred institution, exalted above all utilitarian values; and no matter how benevolent a government is, it may not tamper with them. These rights, however, always remain an idea which can be fulfilled only on condition that the *means* employed to do so are compatible with morality. This limiting condition must not be overstepped by the people, who may not therefore pursue their rights by revolution, which is at all times unjust. The best way of making a nation content with its constitution is to *rule* autocratically and at the same time to *govern* in a republican manner, i.e. to govern in the spirit of republicanism and by analogy with it.

21. A cause whose nature is not directly perceptible can be discovered through the effect which invariably accompanies it. What is an *absolute* monarch? He is one at whose command war at once begins when he says it shall do so. And conversely, what is a *limited* monarch? He is one who must first ask the people whether or not there is to be a war, and if the people say that there shall be no war, then there will be none. For war is a condition in which *all* the powers of the state must be at the head of state's disposal.

Now the monarch of Great Britain has waged numerous wars without asking the people's consent. This king is therefore an absolute monarch, although he should not be so according to the constitution. But he can always bypass the latter, since he can always be assured, by controlling the various powers of the state, that the people's representatives will agree with him; for he has the authority to award all offices and dignities. This corrupt system, however, must naturally be given no publicity if it is to succeed. It therefore remains under a very transparent veil of secrecy.

22. It is certainly *agreeable* to think up political constitutions which meet the requirements of reason (particularly in matters of right). But it is *foolhardy* to put them forward seriously, and *punishable* to incite the people to do away with the existing constitution.

Plato's *Atlantis*, More's *Utopia*, Harrington's *Oceana* and Allais'

Severambia have successively made their appearance, but they have never (with the exception of Cromwell's abortive attempt to establish a despotic republic) been tried out in practice. It is the same with these political creations as with the creation of the world: no one was present at it, nor could anyone have been present, or else he would have been his own creator. It is a pleasant dream to hope that a political product of the sort we here have in mind will one day be brought to perfection, at however remote a date. But it is not merely *conceivable* that we can continually approach such a state; so long as it can be reconciled with the moral law, it is also the *duty* of the head of state (not of the citizens) to do so.

23. The *urge to communicate* must have been the original motive for human beings who were still alone to announce their existence to living creatures outside themselves, especially to those which emit sounds which can be imitated and which can subsequently serve as a name. A similar effect of this urge can still be seen in children and thoughtless people who disturb the thinking section of the community by banging, shouting, whistling, singing and other noisy pastimes (and often even by noisy religious devotions). For I can see no motive for such behaviour other than a desire on the part of those concerned to proclaim their existence to the world at large.

24. The following may be cited as only a few examples of this conflict between man's aspiration towards his moral destiny on the one hand, and his unchanging obedience to laws inherent in his nature and appropriate to a crude and animal condition on the other.

Nature has fixed the time at which human beings reach maturity – in terms of their urge and ability to reproduce their kind – at the age of approximately sixteen or seventeen. This is the age at which, in the raw state of nature, a youth literally becomes a man; for he then has the capacity to look after himself, to reproduce his kind, and to look after his children as well as his wife. The simplicity of his needs makes this an easy task. But in a civilized state, he requires numerous means of support, in terms both of skill and of favourable external circumstances, in order to perform these functions. In the context of civil society, the corresponding stage is therefore postponed – at least on average – by a further ten years. Nevertheless, nature has not altered the age of puberty to match the progressive refinement of society, but sticks stubbornly to the law which it has imposed on the survival of the human race as an animal species. As a result, the effect of social customs on the end of nature – and vice versa – is inevitably prejudicial. For in the state of nature, a human being is already a man at an age when civilized man (who nevertheless still retains his character as natural man) is merely a youth, or even only a child; for we may well describe as a child someone who, in the civil state, is unable because of his age to support even himself, let alone others of his kind, despite having the urge and capacity to produce offspring as called upon by nature. For nature has certainly not endowed living creatures with instincts and capacities in order that they should resist and suppress them. Such abilities were consequently not designed for a state of civilization, but merely for the survival of the human race as an animal species; and the civilized state thus inevitably comes into conflict with the latter, a conflict which only a perfect civil constitution – the ultimate goal of culture – can resolve. Meanwhile, the intervening period [between the state of nature and the state of perfection] is filled as a rule with vices and their consequences, i.e. with human misery in its various forms.

A further example may confirm the truth of the proposition that nature has endowed us with two distinct abilities for two distinct purposes, namely that of man as an animal species and that of man as a moral species. The example in question is the saying of Hippocrates 'ars longa, vita brevis'. The arts and sciences could be advanced much further by one individual with the appropriate talents, once he had attained the necessary maturity of judgement through long practice and the acquisition of knowledge, than by whole generations of scholars in succession, provided that this individual could live and retain his youthful mental capacities for the total lifetimes of the generations in question. Now it is evident that nature has fixed the length of human life with a view to ends other than that of the advancement of the sciences. For just when the most fortunate of thinkers is on the verge of the greatest discoveries which his skill and experience entitle him to expect, old age intervenes; he loses his acuteness and must leave it to the next generation (which starts once more from the ABC and must again traverse the entire distance which had already been covered) to take a further step in the progress of culture. Thus, the course which the human race follows on the way to fulfilling its destiny appears subject to incessant interruptions, with a constant risk of reverting to the original barbarism; and the Greek philosopher had some justification when he complained that *it is a pity that we have to die just when we have begun to realize how we ought to have lived.*

As a third example, we may cite the *inequality* of men – not their inequality in terms of natural gifts or goods bestowed on them by fortune, but it terms of universal *human rights*, about which *Rousseau* complains with a great deal of truth. Yet this inequality is inseparable from culture, so long as the latter proceeds, as it were, without a plan (and this is inevitably the case for a considerable period of time). But it was surely not imposed on man by nature, for nature gave him both freedom and reason, and reason decreed that this freedom is subject to no other limits than those of its own universal and external legality, which is known as *civil right*. Man was meant to rise, by his own efforts, above the barbarism of his natural abilities, but to take care not to contravene them even as he rises above them. He can expect to attain this skill only at a late stage and after many unsuccessful attempts; and in the meantime, the human race groans under the evils which it inflicts on itself as a result of its own inexperience.

25. The *Bedouins* of Arabia still describe themselves as children of a former *sheikh*, the founder of their tribe (such as *Beni Haled* and others). But the sheikh is by no means their *master*, and he cannot force his will upon them as he chooses. For in a nation of herdsmen, no one has fixed property which he cannot take with him, so that any family which is discontented with its tribe can easily leave it and join forces with another.

THE STORY OF PENGUIN CLASSICS

Before 1946 ...'Classics' are mainly the domain of academics and students, without readable editions for everyone else. This all changes when a little-known classicist, E. V. Rieu, presents Penguin founder Allen Lane with the translation of Homer's Odyssey that he has been working on and reading to his wife Nelly in his spare time.

1946 The Odyssey becomes the first Penguin Classic published, and promptly sells three million copies. Suddenly, classic books are no longer for the privileged few.

1950s Rieu, now series editor, turns to professional writers for the best modern, readable translations, including Dorothy L. Sayers's *Inferno* and Robert Graves's *The Twelve Caesars*, which revives the salacious original.

1960s 1961 sees the arrival of the Penguin Modern Classics, showcasing the best twentieth-century writers from around the world. Rieu retires in 1964, hailing the Penguin Classics list as 'the greatest educative force of the 20th century'.

1970s A new generation of translators arrives to swell the Penguin Classics ranks, and the list grows to encompass more philosophy, religion, science, history and politics.

1980s The Penguin American Library joins the Classics stable, with titles such as *The Last of the Mohicans* safeguarded. Penguin Classics now offers the most comprehensive library of world literature available.

1990s Penguin Popular Classics are launched, offering readers budget editions of the greatest works of literature. Penguin Audiobooks brings the classics to a listening audience for the first time, and in 1999 the launch of the Penguin Classics website takes them online to an ever larger global readership.

The 21st Century Penguin Classics are rejacketed for the first time in nearly twenty years. This world famous series now consists of more than 1,300 titles, making the widest range of the best books ever written available to millions – and constantly redefining the meaning of what makes a 'classic'.

The Odyssey continues ...

The best books ever written

PENGUIN (🐧) CLASSICS

SINCE 1946

Find out more at www.penguinclassics.com